Creative development

Planning and Assessment **Stepping Stones** **Early Learning Goals** **Practical activity ideas**

Kevin Kelman and
Susan Smith

British Library Cataloguing-in-Publication Data A catalogue record for this book is available from the British Library.

ISBN 0 439 98352 5

Authors
Kevin Kelman and Susan Smith

Editor
Jane Bishop

Designer
Clare Brewer

Assistant Editor
Victoria Lee

Illustrations
Julie Clough

Series Designer
Clare Brewer

Cover photography
Derek Cooknell

Text © 2003 Kevin Kelman and Susan Smith
© 2003 Scholastic Ltd

Thank you, Paul and Brian, for your continued support.

Designed using Adobe Pagemaker

Published by Scholastic Ltd,
Villiers House,
Clarendon Avenue,
Leamington Spa,
Warwickshire CV32 5PR

Visit our website at www.scholastic.co.uk
Printed by Proost NV, Belgium

1 2 3 4 5 6 7 8 9 0   3 4 5 6 7 8 9 0 1 2

Acknowledgements
Qualifications and Curriculum Authority for the use of extracts from the QCA/DfEE document *Curriculum Guidance for the Foundation Stage* © 2000 Qualifications and Curriculum Authority.
Every effort has been made to trace copyright holders and the publishers apologise for any inadvertent omissions.

The publishers gratefully acknowledge permission to reproduce the following copyright material:
Brenda Williams for the use of 'Round the zoo' by Brenda Williams © 2003, Brenda Williams, previously unpublished.

Contents

Creative development

Chapter 4 — Responding to experiences

Photocopiable pages

Introduction

The six books in this series provide support in planning, teaching and assessing the Foundation Stage curriculum, as outlined in the *Curriculum Guidance for the Foundation Stage* (QCA). Each of the six books covers one of the Areas of Learning with activities based on specific Early Learning Goals and Stepping Stones.

Although this book follows the guidelines set down for the Creative development Area within the *Curriculum Guidance for the Foundation Stage* for England, the activities described can be used equally well within the guidelines for early years in Scotland (in the Expressive and aesthetic development Area of *A Curriculum Framework for Children 3 to 5*), Northern Ireland (in the Creative/Aesthetic development Area of the *Curricular Guidance for Pre-School Education*) and Wales (Creative development Area of the *Outcomes for Children's Learning Before Compulsory School Age*).

Developing artistic skills

The Early Learning Goals for Creative development recommend that children should be given opportunities to develop their imagination, as well as their ability to communicate and express their ideas, thoughts and feelings, through a variety of media. Furthermore, children should be provided with opportunities to respond creatively in a variety of ways to what they see, hear, smell, touch and feel. To achieve these aims, the children should be introduced to a widening range of different resources, materials, implements, instruments and techniques.

The Early Learning Goals state that 'creativity is fundamental to successful learning'. The best approach to nurturing creativity is for the adult to allow the children as much freedom to explore and express themselves as possible, rather than continuously channelling or directing their actions.

It is also worth bearing in mind, when implementing creative activities, that the experiences and processes in which the children participate should remain the primary focus. For this reason, the learning outcomes detailed in the activities in this book should not be seen as set in stone. Instead they should always be viewed as open-ended and open to interpretation by each child.

Providing support

It is important to encourage the children to talk about what they are doing as they work through each stage of the creative process. Remember to give praise to all the children's artistic efforts, not just those seen as perfect to the adult eye.

Creative development

Aim to recognise when it is appropriate to give help and only intervene if absolutely necessary, thus allowing children independence and the opportunity for creativity. If a child has been identified as having specific needs, support should be targeted to meet these requirements. It is important to remember that each activity in this book may be adapted to suit the needs of the individual, in order to ensure that every child has a sense of achievement.

How to use this book

This book is aimed at early years practitioners working in a variety of settings. The activities are suitable for playgroups and other voluntary groups, childminders, private provision, local authority nurseries and classes or parents.

There are four activity chapters, each covering one of the clusters of Early Learning Goals for Creative development: Exploring media and materials; Music; Imagination, and Responding to experiences, and expressing and communicating ideas.

The activity chapters provide several suggested activities for each of the Stepping Stones for Creative development. For easy reference, the Stepping Stones for each activity have been colour-coded, with activities at the simplest level shaded yellow, those in the middle shaded blue and the more difficult shaded green, to match the colours used to show progression in the *Curriculum Guidance for the Foundation Stage*.

Within each chapter, the activities are grouped with the earlier Stepping Stones (shown in yellow) coming first and the later Stepping Stones (shown in green) towards the end of the chapter. Although these are organised in a hierarchical order, children's development does not necessarily follow such smooth patterns, and this book is not designed to be systematically followed page by page.

Each activity is presented in a uniform way with guidance on materials that are needed and step-by-step instructions for the activity with the final statements providing suggestions for supporting and challenging children, depending on their level of development.

'More ideas' provides further alternative suggestions for achieving the same Stepping Stone, and 'Other curriculum areas' shows how the same objective can be achieved across other Areas of Learning. 'Home links' suggests ways of involving parents and carers in their children's education and development.

Other areas of the curriculum

Although Creative development is outlined as a specific Area of Learning, to help practitioners plan activities and experiences, this should not be interpreted to mean that children's learning is divided into distinct segments. Instead, practitioners should see the Areas of Learning as being guidelines and should recognise that the experiences and activities that the children have will further their development in a variety of skills, concepts and abilities that span several Areas of Learning.

For example, children working on a large-scale piece of outdoor weaving (see 'Hessian art' on page 36) will be involved in working together and sharing equipment (Personal, social and emotional development), finding out and talking about their natural environment (Knowledge and understanding of the world), comparing lengths and thicknesses of different materials (Mathematical development) and using gross motor and fine manipulative skills to physically create their own design (Physical development).

Home links

It is vital to establish and maintain good lines of communication with the child's home setting so that parents and carers are an integral part of the learning that takes place. It is important to inform the people within the children's homes of some of the activities in which their child is taking part and to gain their support by encouraging involvement. Each activity in this book includes home-link suggestions so that parents and carers can be involved in their child's learning.

Photocopiable sheets

Eighteen sheets are provided on pages 79–96, which can be photocopied and used for planning and assessment purposes, to support the main activities, to provide stimulus for the activities or to enhance the home links that are an important feature within this book.

Planning and assessment

As with all areas of the curriculum, when you are planning a Creative development programme, it is vital to ensure a wide range of activities that allow for continuity and progression in the children's learning. Chapter 1 of this book provides advice and guidance on ways to ensure effective planning.

Adults play an essential role in supporting children's learning and gathering evidence of their capabilities. The information that is gathered about a child's progress will be used to ensure continuity and further progression in their learning. A guide to assessment and record keeping can be found in Chapter 2.

© JAMES LEVIN/SODA

Equal opportunities

It is important to provide activities in which all children can participate and benefit equally from. Children with special needs, for example, can benefit greatly from activities that focus on listening, touching and movement.

Many aspects of Creative development provide a wealth of different opportunities for children to experience the diversity of our multicultural society. Their horizons will be broadened and their experiences enriched if you offer the children resources, for example, musical instruments, costumes, artwork, stories and dance, from around the globe. Activities should provide free rein for the child's imagination and not be bounded by gender stereotyping. Experiences should be available for all children regardless of their gender, personality or ability, and the children should feel able to express their creativity in their own way.

Creating displays

The environment of an early years setting should be stimulating, motivating and interesting for the children. Displaying the children's work effectively can be the key to giving the children a real sense of achievement from what they have produced.

To ensure that each child and their parents and carers feel part of your early years' community, displays should involve work from every child. Consideration should be given to the positioning of displays so that where possible they can be used as an interactive resource. Displays also

provide opportunities for the children to observe and show appreciation for the work of others. A child's expression of art should be valued and displayed in the exact form it was made, rather than being adapted to fit an adult's idea of what it should look like.

Provide opportunities for the children to perform songs and dance to an audience as this not only constitutes a form of display, but also provides a learning experience in itself. It is relatively easy to display artwork and models, however to 'display' these other creative activities, such as dance and music-making, you will need to make recordings using a camera, camcorder or tape recorder. Encourage parents and carers to use these on your behalf at special events or the children's performances.

Involving artists

Consider inviting a professional artist, musician or craftsperson in to your setting to provide the children with an exciting stimulus for their own creative development. Start by asking parents, grandparents or carers if any have a creative talent and some time to spare.

Your local authority may have an education officer who can provide you with relevant contacts for local working artists; ask about any grants that may be available to support such initiatives. To make events more feasible it is worthwhile working with other local, early years groups so that you can all benefit from this valuable resource. The Musician's Union (tel: 020-7582 5566) may be able to locate local musicians who could visit your group.

Keep a look out for suitable drama experiences for your children such as touring theatre groups who aim performances at early years groups. Taking children to see productions can provide a rich learning experience for them. Contact local drama companies to find individuals who are prepared to come and talk to the children, show costumes, run mini workshops on mime or make-up, or perform for them.

Planning

The Foundation Stage curriculum is organised into six Areas of Learning which help practitioners to plan appropriate activities and experiences for the children they are working with. However, the *Curriculum Guidance for the Foundation Stage* document states, 'This does not mean that all of young children's learning is divided up into areas. One experience may provide a child with opportunities to develop a number of competencies and concepts across several areas of learning.' Practitioners need to focus continually on this when planning for learning.

Partners in planning

Planning for the Foundation Stage will be most effective when it is directly linked with assessment, celebrating children's learning and achievements, and looking forward to the next steps in learning.

Everyone involved in working with the children should be included in planning. By using a team approach, staff can feed their ideas and observations into the planning process, giving everyone a sense of ownership over the plans and this can result in members of a team feeling more motivated when implementing new plans. Those who contribute to the planning process will have a clearer picture of its aims and this will ensure a consistent approach.

Successful planning can ensure that children follow a broad and balanced curriculum that allows for the progression of each child. However, opportunities for child-initiated play should be allowed for in curriculum planning, and activities should have built-in flexibility to cater for individual interests, needs or spontaneity to give children a sense of ownership in their learning.

Strengthen and extend this sense of ownership by involving the children in the planning process, by:
- asking the children which toys and equipment they would like in the water or sand tray this week
- sharing catalogues with the children and asking for their suggestions when you order new materials
- reviewing the day with the children and asking what they would like to continue with tomorrow
- discussing the children's plans for the day ahead and the areas in which they would like to play.

Involving parents and carers

Share your planning with parents and carers, particularly where they work alongside practitioners as parent helpers. In such circumstances the parent should be clear on exactly what is expected of them and how much input is required. For example, you will need to inform the helper supervising a cut and stick activity, that the cutting does not have to be perfectly accurate, or that sticking in a cluster is acceptable.

© JOHN FORTUNATO/SODA

Creative development

Display your plans on a notice-board and add to home links by encouraging learning to be extended at home and by giving parents and carers opportunities to contribute resources, knowledge and expertise, where appropriate.

Practical examples of this may include:

■ informing parents that the children have been listening to some classical music and encouraging parents to play further pieces for their children at home

■ inviting parents to share a skill with their children, for example, line dancing, Morris dancing or Scottish country dancing

■ encouraging parents to sign up to accompany their children on a sensory walk or trip to the theatre.

In this way parents should feel there is an open dialogue for them to contribute or make suggestions towards their child's learning.

Practitioners may need to plan opportunities to encourage parents and carers to value the creative processes that their children go through, as well as the results they achieve. Often, parents and carers may only value the end product of the many processes a child has experienced.

Equal opportunities

All children are entitled to the same curriculum, regardless of their gender, racial origin, cultural background or ability. An effective implementation of equal opportunities would be to ensure that positive steps are taken to remove barriers to achieve this objective.

Creative development is an effective vehicle to develop multicultural awareness. Children should have access to equipment, books and music that reflect the communities in which they live and which represent different cultures and languages. Opportunities in role-play, drama and dance provide platforms for children to experience and use artefacts that reflect and celebrate diversity. These will stimulate children to think in different ways. Practitioners should also account for traditions, for example, Islamic art uses patterns, not representations of people or animals.

The range of resources provided for the activities should encourage both boys and girls to take up a variety of roles and to participate equally. Stereotypical attitudes should be challenged through creative activities by providing adults as positive gender role models, for example, inviting a father to role-play a nurse in the role-play area. As far as possible inhibitions caused by comments from other children or adults should be eliminated. Parental co-operation is of enormous importance if this is to be achieved.

The Creative development activities in this book are flexible enough to be adapted to cater for specific needs in social, physical, emotional and linguistic development. Aspects of Creative development, such as music and sensory experiences, enable most children to take part and achieve enjoyment, regardless of their individual needs.

Physical adaptations may be necessary to ensure that children with physical disabilities gain equal access to activities. Just as children with developmental delays need help and encouragement to use every opportunity to foster their learning, more able children also need to be challenged and enabled to advance their learning at an appropriate pace.

Long-, medium- and short-term planning

Plans need to be closely linked to the Areas of Learning and should provide clear information about what the children will do and what the children are expected to learn. Staff should make effective use of assessment information to identify individual children's needs and plan the next steps in their learning. Plan should be evaluated and adjusted accordingly to meet the changing needs of the children.

Although written plans are a necessary feature of early years provision, the pivotal aspect is the process itself. Planning should be used as a tool to build on prior learning and the knowledge that the children have gained through previous experience, and plans should be viewed as a set of working documents.

There are three components to effective planning, although some establishments may find two of these to be sufficient.

Long-term plans

These provide a broad overview of the Early Learning Goals relating to all six Areas of Learning. Consider seasonal variations when you choose which themes you will use to deliver the curriculum.

The Stepping Stones are designed to be used with children from the age of three through to the end of the Foundation Stage. You will need to consider how much of this time the children will spend in your setting, and to plan accordingly. It may be necessary to devise a two-year rolling programme for Creative development if the children are to be in your setting for more than a year.

Long-term plans should include when you intend to teach Areas of Learning, how regularly and frequently you want to teach them and how you will achieve this in a relevant and interesting way. Include special events and activities such as visits or festivals.

Medium-term plans

More detailed than long-term plans, and in many settings related to a theme approach, medium-term planning may cover a period such as a term.

For Creative development, you may choose to identify a specific focus for learning each term, from the categories of art, music, dance, role-play and imaginative play. In addition, all aspects of creative development should be provided for on a regular basis, to enhance the children's skills and to ensure their continuing development in each area.

© JAMES LEVIN/SODA

Creative development

Short-term plans

The most detailed plans may be weekly or daily and they should be based on a working knowledge of the Stepping Stones and Early Learning Goals. Short-term planning should remain flexible so that it can take account of the children's ideas and their responses to learning experiences and can allow learning to develop spontaneously. For example, when the weather changes and it has started to snow outdoors or a child in the group has a new baby born into the family.

Structure does not have to mean routines and continuous adult-led activity. When a plan has been adapted, subsequent plans should be reviewed to ensure that breadth and balance of learning is assured. In doing so, learning at the Foundation Stage should continue to be influenced by and responsive to the children's learning within a context of a long-term plan. At the end of a week, you can assess which activities should be extended or offered again the week after.

Short-term plans for the Foundation Stage will provide clear learning objectives based on the Stepping Stones and Early Learning Goals. The plans should consist of a brief description of the activities and how these can be adapted for individual or groups of children. They should take account of how the children will be organised, the role of the adults (including parents and carers) and any resources and equipment needed.

A creative learning environment

As well as planning an interesting range of activities for Creative development, it is also important to give careful consideration to setting up a rich play environment.

It is essential that creative play should not be viewed as an 'extra' that children are allowed to participate in when the more important things have been completed. Creative skills are central to the children's all-round development and should be part of a carefully planned provision in all areas of an early years setting, in order to help the children to learn across the six Areas of Learning.

When planning for the day, make sure that you provide a balance of adult-led and child-initiated activities. Resources play a significant role in all these activities, in that they help facilitate children's learning. Adults must remember that activities should be offered but never imposed on children. When children are involved in creative activities, the learning that takes place may differ from what was expected. Therefore, all learning, whether planned or unplanned, that occurs during creative play is valid.

To maximise on opportunities for child-initiated learning, aim to store creative materials so that the children can easily access them. They should be at the children's height and clearly labelled with both words and pictures.

Consider your provision for opportunities for creative development within each of the popular play areas listed here.

Sand
■ Vary the texture – provide dry sand, wet sand, add pebbles and other materials to it.
■ Provide other materials in the sand tray, such as flour, lentils, soil, sawdust, shredded paper, tissue paper, pasta, dried peas, peat, compost, bark, beans or tea leaves.
■ Include equipment such as sieves, plastic buckets, plastic cups, tubs, rakes, scoops, spades, plastic shapes, funnels, moulds, diggers and trowels.
■ Encourage children to add shells, seaweed and small-world toys to their creations in the sand tray.

Water
■ Compare the sounds made with water, using equipment such as sponges, watering cans, various sizes and shapes of plastic containers, pourers, washing-up liquid containers, plastic bottles, sieves, toy pumps, funnels, tubes, measuring spoons and droppers.
■ Look at the texture of different materials, such as cotton wool, sponges and various fabrics, both when they are dry and then when they are wet.
■ Vary contents of the water tray by adding bubbles, food colouring, ice cubes, warm water, a bath bomb, petals or corks.

Role-play
Adapt your basic home corner to suit a wide range of creative themes. Try to ensure that a selection of multicultural items related to the theme are included where appropriate.
■ The Wedding Shop – set out tables, chairs, hats, clothes, mirror, telephone, books, magazines, posters, photographs, writing paper, pencils, crayons and an appointment book.
■ In the Kitchen – provide cutlery, bowls, plates, chopsticks, baltis, woks, trays, towels, play food such as baguettes, chapattis, tortillas, bagels and naan bread, and cookbooks.

Outdoor play
■ Playground or pavement pictures – use chalks, pastels and water.
■ Movement and dance activities around a makeshift maypole, using ribbons, kites or a parachute.
■ Create an outdoor exploration role-play area or den using sheets, garden canes, clothes pegs and so on, which will enable the children to think imaginatively and explore ideas of space.

ICT
■ Use tape recorders and microphones during musical activities.
■ Provide simple drawing software to allow children to create artwork.
■ Include cameras for the children to record each other's expressions and creations.

Creative development

Small-world play
■ Provide a range of puppets with a puppet theatre, include hand puppets, finger puppets, sock puppets and paper plate puppets.
■ Include play animals, vehicles and people to create a dinosaur world, a farm, a street scene or a jungle.

© DAN HOWELL/SODA

Art and craft
To enable the children to have freedom in their creativity, provide as wide a range of resources as possible. Consider some of the following:
■ Vary the base material that the children use, providing paper of various textures, sizes and thicknesses, real clay, play dough, egg-boxes, cereal boxes, yoghurt cartons, round cheese boxes, styrofoam trays, plastic bottles, toothpaste boxes, wallpaper, corrugated card, hessian sack, polystyrene squares and smooth pebbles.
■ Vary the mark-makers that children use, include pencils of different hardness, thicknesses and colours; different brushes (toothbrush, bottle brush, scrubbing brush, make-up brush, pasting brush); rollers; paints in different shades, colours and consistencies; face paints; finger paints; chalks; charcoal; crayons from wax to those which can be blended or mixed with water; felt-tipped pens (non-toxic and washable); pastels.
■ Provide a wide range of collage materials and textures, such as glitter, shiny shapes, sticky shapes, lollipop sticks, scraps of material, sawdust, seeds, twigs, straw, wrapping paper, rice, bottle tops, pasta, straws, pencil shavings, netting, string, scraps of foil, pipe-cleaners and feathers.

Natural discovery
■ Take sensory walks in the garden, park, forest, to the supermarket, at the beach.
■ Match colour squares to natural materials found outside, such as grasses, leaves, flowers, trees, rocks and soil.
■ Collect natural materials to use for collages, making prints or creating a texture board.

Construction
■ Design structures using DUPLO, LEGO, Brio and Sticklebricks.
■ Use the construction materials to create instruments which the children can play.

Malleable materials
■ Children enjoy being able to roll, shape, cut, stretch, throw, knead and pummel malleable materials. Adapt the basic recipes on page 81 to vary the experience.
■ Use malleable materials to create items for the role-play area, such as food stuffs, jewellery, bowls and so on.
■ Add smelly essences such as vanilla, peppermint, strawberry and lemon, or texture such as glitter, sand, petals, sawdust, pasta or lentils, to different types of dough.

Creative development

Assessment

Every good early years practitioner will be assessing their children during every session in the group. This will include informal observations and interactions with the children as they play as well as a more formal, systematic approach. Together these assessments will build up a picture of each child's development and will enable the practitioner to recognise the next steps in planning for them.

The importance of assessment

Assessment is necessary for practitioners to:
- find out what a child knows and identify their individual needs
- ensure that individual needs are addressed in future planning
- gain evidence of an individual child's progress
- identify when a child has success and where they have difficulty
- recognise when to offer support or encourage independence
- evaluate the effectiveness of the learning environment, including learning, teaching and resources
- record and share information with colleagues, parents and other agencies, if necessary.

When to assess?

Make an initial assessment of each child when they join your group. On enrolment, give parents and carers a simple questionnaire that will help you to ascertain the child's current stage of development, favourite activities and previous learning experience. Questions that you could ask about Creative development could include:

- Can the child hold a pencil?
- What is the child's favourite song?
- Does the child enjoy 'pretend' play?

Attached to this questionnaire could be a simple sheet which children can complete, with parental support, to record the kinds of activities they enjoy.

After this initial introduction to the group, both informal and formal assessment will be ongoing. You will need to work as a team to plan and follow a systematic approach to ensure that each child is regularly assessed in each area of Creative development – art, music, dance, role-play and imaginative play. At the same time, the value of on-the-spot observations should not be forgotten, and every effort should be made to jot these down for future reference.

Who will assess?

Systematic observation and information gathering will work best when all practitioners involved with the children act as a team, rather than as individuals. Teamwork will enable a realistic amount of time to be set aside and will allow observations and information gathering to take place.

Creative development

Assessment

■ Allocate time for an adult to focus on an individual activity or on specific children for a period of time, to gather information that can then be shared with other people.

■ Alternatively, key worker systems allow an adult to take responsibility for observing a specific group of children across all Areas of Learning.

Provision should also be made for information from other adults working in the setting, parents, students and so on, to feed specific observations back to staff at the end of the sessions.

Methods of assessment

The many different forms of assessment that early years practitioners can use each have their own merits and there will be times when one method is more suitable than others. Consider the range of methods and vary them accordingly.

Initial profiles of achievement, described on page 15, may include information on the child's initial stage of development across the different areas of Creative development, for example, 'Daisy only recognises the colour yellow'.

Informal observations

On-the-spot observations will provide brief notes recorded at the time of observation and dated. These informal records focus on what the children do rather than what they cannot do yet. The notes will be, by nature, brief and will act as memory aids for more detailed assessment records. Some practitioners find it useful to carry a small notebook for this purpose. Alternatively, a pad of Post-it notes can be used and individual notes can be stuck directly into the child's profile, for example, 'Krupa made up her own song today while playing with the bricks'.

Checklists

Checklists provide a quick and easy record of the child's progress, but they do not give a description or explanation of what the child did, and in which context they achieved it. However, they can be helpful as a reminder of the range of factors to be taken into account in each area of Creative development.

Formal observations

Formal observations differ from on-the-spot observations. They are planned for and time has to be allocated to allow practitioners to build up an accurate indication of the child's progress in one specified area. These observations must be selective and focused for a particular purpose. The practitioner carrying out the observation should not be involved with the child in their activity. They may consider, for example, can the child use one object to represent another, even when the objects have few characteristics in common?

Talking and interacting with the children as they carry out an activity is a good way to gather further information. Ask open-ended questions, for

example, 'Can you tell me about your picture?' or 'Why did you choose that shape for your model?'.

Recording assessments
Samples of work
Keep a folder for each child to store samples of work from across all areas of Creative development. Date and add relevant comments to each sheet. Aim to gather representative samples of the child's work in each area, for example, painting, over a period of time to act as evidence of progress made. Allow children to become involved in selecting pieces of their work for the folder. Each time you add a piece to the collection, take time to discuss with the child their progress in order to enhance their sense of pride and achievement. Where work cannot be stored, for example, 3-D models or using instruments, take photographs and place these in the folder along with relevant comments and the date instead.

Photographs of activities
While it is easy to photograph examples of individual children's work, photographs of group activities, such as in 'Hessian art' (page 36) or 'Listen and move' (page 47), that show the involvement of several children, can be used for summative assessments and displayed for parents and carers on open nights and at other events.

Tape recordings and video recordings
In addition to individual folders it may sometimes be useful to record the children talking through their activity or singing, or to video-tape a session in the role-play area. Use these recordings to assess the children's progress in these areas and play them on open evenings or to parents and carers at sessions where you are reporting back to them on their child's progress.

Foundation Stage Profile
In January 2003, the Qualifications and Curriculum Authority introduced a new assessment document for early years practitioners working within the Foundation Stage. The *Foundation Stage Profile* provides a 12-page document to be completed for each child throughout the Foundation Stage. Within it the curriculum is broken down to provide assessment for all six Areas of Learning with nine 'targets' for Creative development.

Written records
Each setting may also use its own methods for keeping written records on each child's development. These focus on results and outcomes and are often used at the transition stage to identify what a child can do

'now'. These records can be relatively detailed, to give accurate information on the child's current stage of development, and are written up using previous assessments made over a period of time. These can be used to pass information about each child to their parents and carers or staff at settings where the child is moving on to. Use the record sheet on page 79 in this book to record the children's progress in Creative development.

Assessment for planning

The observations you make and the samples of work you collect will provide evidence of a child's skills. To make an assessment, you will need to evaluate the evidence you have gathered in order to make informed judgements about a child's development and learning.

When you do this, consider what information you want to collect and why, who will collect the information, when and how often the information will be collected, how much detail is required, whether the information needs to be summarised or categorised and how it will be recorded.

Using assessment information

Use the results of your assessments for future planning. You should aim to develop plans based on where the child is now and what the next steps should be, matching the child's development to the Stepping Stones in Creative development as the children work towards the Early Learning Goal.

Next, you should put your plans into action, carrying out planned assessments and informal observations to evaluate progress made, highlight strengths and pinpoint development needs. Finally analyse your findings and modify future plans.

Adjusting your methods

By following this cycle you may find areas where skills are not being developed. For example, if a child never visits the role-play area, this whole area of Creative development may be neglected. Once you are aware of this you can alter a short-term plan and, for example, ask the child to suggest what they would like the area to be set up as (for example, hospital, shop or vet's). You can then plan for that child to be involved in helping to set up and then playing in the area throughout the following week.

Parents and carers

It is important to keep parents and carers informed of their child's progress by listening to their comments and views, sharing the children's work with them, alerting them to any concerns, suggesting ways they can help with their child's learning and development at home and providing opportunities for them to inform staff of the child's achievements outside the group. In addition, there can also be open days or evenings, formal reports and parents' evenings.

When encouraging young children to explore media and materials, adults should act as providers rather than controllers, to allow the children to use their imagination freely and create their own individual pieces of work.

Match that colour

What to do
■ Gather the children in a small circle and read *Elmer's Colours*.
■ Next, scatter the squares of coloured felt around the room. Choose one child to point to one of the squares on Elmer's coat in the book and choose another child to find the corresponding felt square in the room.
■ Sit back in your circle and give each child a small square of colour from a DIY paint sample. Ask the children, one at a time, to find an item in the room that matches their colour square.
■ Play 'Colour jack-in-the-box' with the children as they sit in a circle, by giving each child a new colour sample and placing a collection of items of clothing, books and toys in the middle of the circle. If a child can see the same colour as their sample in the collection they can jump up and shout 'My colour's in the sock!' or 'My colour's in the train!' and so on.
■ With younger children place a basket of coloured socks and gloves in the centre of the circle and invite the children to match the pairs.
■ Take older children on a colour search asking them to find as many red things within a certain amount of time. Repeat with other colours.

More ideas
■ Invite the children to paint Elmer's colours using ready-mixed paint and applying it using cotton buds, shoe polish applicators or empty roll-on deodorant bottles.
■ Use squares of felt or sticky-backed paper to make collages of Elmer. Encourage the children to name the colours on the squares.

Other curriculum areas
PSED   Pass a coloured beanbag around at circle time and invite the children to say whether they are wearing the colour in their clothes today. Repeat with beanbags in different colours.

PD   Play a simple game using coloured hoops randomly placed around an open space. Invite the children to run around until you call out a colour when they should run to, and stand in, a hoop of that colour.

Home links
Ask parents and carers to draw their children's attention to different colours at home, such as plants in the garden, foods in the kitchen and so on.

Patchwork quilt

Early Learning Goal
Explore colour, texture, shape, form and space in two or three dimensions.

Group size
Up to ten children.

What you need
Squares measuring 50 x 50cm of the following materials: bubble wrap, linoleum, hessian sack, carpet, laminate flooring, felt, fake fur, thick textured wallpaper, sandpaper, denim, leather, silk, rubber, cork tiling, LEGO base board, holographic paper; large roll of good quality tape; small bag containing a 5cm x 5cm square of a selection of the pieces of material listed.

Preparation
Secure the squares of different materials in a random pattern together to form a large patchwork quilt, using the roll of tape.

What to do
■ Gather the children in a circle and place the ready-made 'quilt' in the centre of the group.
■ Allow the children to explore the textures of the quilt using their hands and feet, inviting them to crawl and roll over it one at a time, and encourage them to describe the different textures.
■ Invite the children in turn to reach into the small bag and to select one of the small squares of material. Without removing it from the bag ask the child to describe the texture and to say which of the large squares in the quilt it matches.
■ Let younger children remove the small squares from the bag to match them to the larger squares.
■ Ask older children to make rubbings of some of the different textures using white paper and wax crayons. Laminate these and see if the children can match the rubbings to the textures.

More ideas
■ Cut up small pieces of materials and invite the children to use them to make texture collages.
■ Make a large Humpty Dumpty collage using different textures of material for the bricks.

Other curriculum areas
MD Make some texture dominoes for the children to match.
KUW Look closely at the textures and patterns of features of the local environment, such as trees, brick walls and wire mesh on a pet's hutch.

Home links
Invite parents to make a list of different textured items the children have been able to find in the house, in the car, in the park and so on.

Dinosaur land

What to do
■ Look at the different types of dinosaurs in the books together and discuss their distinguishing features, for example, a Stegosaurus has a long neck and a Pterodactyl has wings.
■ Provide the children with a range of recycled modelling materials and equipment that will allow them to cut, join and finish off their models to build their dinosaurs.
■ Encourage the children to work together in pairs to select materials to make a dinosaur.
■ Show them how to fold a paper plate in half to make a head for a Triceratops or a back for a Stegosaurus, simply gluing the plate in half and cutting a wavy line around it.
■ When the children's 3-D structures are dry, allow the children to paint them with a mixture of poster paint and PVA glue.
■ Provide help for younger children to enable them to join the different parts of their structures together.
■ Challenge older children to see if they can make moving parts on their models, such as the head, legs or wings.

More ideas
■ Create a prehistoric landscape for the dinosaurs outdoors using compost, rocks, pebbles, twigs, moss and leaves.
■ Use rocks, pebbles and pipe-cleaners to make dinosaurs, for example, sticking 'googly eyes' (pebbles) to the 'dinosaurs' (rocks) with PVA glue. Add fake fur and acrylic paints to create other features.

Other curriculum areas
KUW   Log on to www.enchantedlearning.com/subjects/dinosaurs to find out more about dinosaurs' features before building and painting the models.

MD   Read *Ten Little Dinosaurs* by Paul Stickland (Ragged Bears) to help develop the children's counting skills. Invite the children to make ten small 3-D dinosaurs using play dough.

Stepping Stone
Make three-dimensional structures.

Early Learning Goal
Explore colour, texture, shape, form and space in two or three dimensions.

Group size
Up to six children.

What you need
Recycled materials for modelling, such as tubes, containers of various shapes, plastic bottles, cotton reels, card, paper plates, cardboard and so on; joining equipment such as scissors, masking tape, adhesive, treasury tags, paper fasteners; poster paints mixed with PVA glue; information books and posters that contain pictures of different types of dinosaurs.

Home links
Suggest that parents and carers visit the library to choose information books about dinosaurs with their children.

Mono prints

Stepping Stone
Differentiate marks
and movements on
paper.

**Early Learning
Goal**
Explore colour,
texture, shape, form
and space in two or
three dimensions.

Group size
Up to ten children.

What you need
Aprons; ink rollers;
water-based ink;
laminated table-top;
cotton buds;
feathers; twigs;
cocktail sticks; large
sheets of newspaper.

Home links
Provide parents and
carers with an
information sheet on
simple printing
techniques that can
be used at home,
such as making mesh
vegetable bag prints
by placing foam or
cotton wool inside
onion bags and using
them to print directly
on to paper.

What to do

■ Ask the children to put on aprons and invite them to roll some of the ink evenly on to the table-top.

■ Allow the children to experiment by making different marks with their fingers in the ink. Encourage them to create waves, spirals, jagged lines, dotted lines and straight lines in the ink.

■ Help the children to carefully place a piece of newsprint over the inked area, to smooth the paper over the ink and to peel it off to reveal their print.

■ Extend the activity to allow the children to make different marks in the ink using cotton buds, feathers, twigs or cocktail sticks.

■ Display the children's prints and discuss the different types of marks.

■ Use two or more colours of ink and vary the colours of paper used for making the print.

■ Allow younger children to squirt shaving foam, which is easier to manipulate, on to a laminated table-top and make marks in the foam.

■ Challenge older children to make pictures in the ink, asking them if they can draw a house with a garden or a family in the car and so on.

More ideas

■ Use other printing techniques using fruit and vegetables, Sticklebricks or cotton reels to make prints.

■ Dip a corn-on-the-cob into a shallow tray of ink and roll it over a sheet of paper to create an interesting print.

Other curriculum areas

KUW Show the children how a photocopier works and take an exact 'print' of one of their pieces of work.

CLL Cut out letters from sponge and use them to print on sheets of newspaper. Call out a letter and ask the children to circle as many examples of it as they can.

Mysterious marks

What to do

■ Invite the children to join you at the table covered with the lining paper and ask them to start carefully rubbing the lining paper with wax crayons.

■ Observe the children's reactions as marks appear on the paper where the items are taped underneath.

■ Provide the children with sheets of paper to explore other textures that make marks on paper.

■ Demonstrate to the children how they can work in pairs to take rubbings. One child should hold the paper firmly in place over the surface, while their partner rubs with a wax crayon lengthways over the paper to create an impression.

■ Allow the children to explore and experiment by rubbing different textures using some of the larger items listed in 'What you need'.

■ Encourage younger children to rub hard enough to make a good impression on the paper.

■ Older children can play a game trying to match the rubbing to the texture from which it was originally taken.

More ideas

■ Use wax candles instead of wax crayons to make rubbings. Coat the candle rubbings with thin, water-based paint to see the 'magic' texture emerging.

■ Make wax-resist pictures by completely covering a small square of paper with different colours of wax crayons. Coat this with a mixture of black poster paint and washing-up liquid. When dry, the children can use cocktail sticks to draw a picture on top of the black coating that will come off to reveal multicoloured lines.

Other curriculum areas

KUW Go outdoors with the children to take some environmental rubbings from different features in the local area, such as paving stones, house name plaques, letterboxes and so on.

PSED Let the children take rubbings from coins. Attach some ribbon to the rubbings and make medals that can be presented to children who have been particularly helpful or friendly.

Home links

Ask parents and carers to make rubbings at home with their children from tool boxes, kitchen drawers and toy cupboards.

Stepping Stone
Differentiate marks and movements on paper.

Early Learning Goal
Explore colour, texture, shape, form and space in two or three dimensions.

Group size
Up to ten children.

What you need
Jumbo wax crayons (wrappers removed); double-sided sticky tape; roll of lining paper; sheets of A4 paper; small squares of sandpaper, material and fabric; leaves; coins; plastic knives; plastic shapes; large items to take rubbings from, such as embossed wallpaper, soles of shoes, lace and doilies, combs, corrugated cardboard, bubble wrap, shopping baskets, colanders, and plastic and polystyrene food trays.

Preparation
Secure a range of the small flat objects listed above to a table-top with double-sided sticky tape. Cover the table-top with thin lining paper and tape it in place.

Texture trove

Early Learning Goal
Explore colour, texture, shape, form and space in two or three dimensions.

Group size
Up to ten children.

What you need
An old hamper or basket; wide range of textured items, such as pasta, pebbles, beads, dried seeds, twigs, tissues, wool, cotton wool, sponges, felt, old towels and corrugated cardboard; bath towel; sheet of sandpaper.

Preparation
Fill an old hamper or wicker basket (or make a cardboard treasure chest) with a range of textured objects.

Home links
Make a list of things for a family to try to find over a weekend, for example, four prickly items, an item that is rough and smooth, a slippery thing, two hairy items and so on.

What to do
■ Ask the children to come and sit in a circle and place the hamper or treasure chest in the centre of the group.
■ Invite the children to explore the contents of the container, describing how each item feels and describing the different textures using their developing vocabulary.
■ Introduce the children to any new relevant words, such as soft, hard, prickly, smooth, spiky, furry, shiny, rough, flat, lumpy, stretchy, crinkly, jagged, fluffy and bumpy.
■ Explain to the children that you want them to make a textured collage.
■ Invite them to work together in pairs to create a collage that is soft, hard, rough or smooth. Provide large pieces of material for the base to create the collage on, for example, a bath towel for a soft collage or a large piece of sandpaper for a rough collage and then allow the children to place relevant items on top of it to make their own creation.

■ Provide younger children with items that can all be described as soft to make a collage, rather than expecting them to sort through the different materials to distinguish textures.
■ Offer older children opportunities to fold, pleat, twist, scrunch, crumple, tear, punch and concertina different papers to change their textures.

More ideas
■ Talk about opposites, such as hot and cold. Warm shaving foam in the microwave for the children (check the temperature before giving it to the children) to explore or add ice cubes to the water tray.
■ Play guessing games by blindfolding the children and asking them to name fruit and vegetables in a basket from touch.

Other curriculum areas
CLL	Make a book of textures by sticking on squares of material and writing describing words below each texture.
MD	Cut out shapes in pieces of card and stick different textures on for the children to explore.

Creative development

Box of lines

What to do

■ Gather the children together in a circle and place the filled gift box in the centre of the group.

■ Draw the children's attention to the box and encourage them to guess what might be inside.

■ Invite one of the children to open the lid and to inspect the contents.

■ Encourage each child to retrieve a 'line' from the box and to take it back to where they are sitting in the group.

■ Ask the children if lines are always straight, then invite them to make a straight line with the piece that they took from the box. Next, encourage them to make a wavy line, followed by a curved line, a zigzag line, or a shape made by joining the ends together. Ask the children to make thick lines and thin lines, too.

Other curriculum areas

CLL Create a story using different types of lines, for example, 'I went for a walk in the snow with my football boots on (draw small dotted lines), I saw sled tracks (draw thin parallel lines) and a bicycle (draw thin curvy lines)'. Ask the children to make up line stories of their own.

KUW Use drawing packages on the computer to make lines and shapes.

■ Instruct younger children to make something specific, such as a tree, a sun, a face and so on.

■ Give older children a set number of 'lines' and ask them to incorporate every single 'line' into a creation of their own choice.

More ideas

■ Cut out clothes shapes from paper and invite the children to use black felt-tipped pens to create different types of lines on them.

■ Draw lines and shapes in different textures, such as shaving foam, wet sand, compost or gloop (see recipe on the photocopiable sheet 'Gloop and papier mâché' on page 80).

Lines in nature

What to do

■ Look at the information books available together and draw the children's attention to lines in nature.

■ Put on coats and outdoor clothing and gather extra adult helpers ready for a walk outdoors to look at natural lines.

■ On your walk draw the children's attention to natural lines so that they understand what they are looking for. Look out for lines in reflections on water and shadows created by the sun.

■ Invite the children to make lines and shapes with the natural objects outdoors. For example, they could make a line of stones or leaves, then they could make shapes or pictures with the same stones or leaves.

■ Use a magnifying glass or viewfinder to look closely at the lines on a piece of wood or on a rock.

■ Encourage the children to take photographs, using a digital or ordinary camera, of natural lines that they cannot bring back to the building.

■ Collect some natural items in an empty margarine tub to take back to your setting, for example, twigs, grasses (long and short), seeds, pebbles, feathers, pine needles and so on.

■ On your return indoors use the 'lines' gathered to make pictures. Encourage the children to make shapes with the materials collected and to glue these on to activity paper using PVA glue.

■ Younger children may require help to cut or snap the materials collected to an appropriate size.

■ Challenge older children to record the lines created by the shadows of trees by placing a piece of paper on the shadow and drawing round it.

More ideas

■ Make lines from play dough and use these to make shapes and pictures.

■ Bend pipe-cleaners to make different shapes.

Other curriculum areas

MD Arrange the natural lines in order of length or thickness. Use the different thicknesses to make a thick square, a thin triangle and so on.

PD Encourage the children to make lines and shapes in the air by moving their fingers, arms, nose, feet and so on.

Home links
Ask parents and carers to help their child to find examples of natural lines in their gardens at home.

I can be an architect!

What to do
■ Gather the children and discuss the different jobs that people do, using the books and posters available to stimulate the discussion. Encourage the children to understand that women and men have equal opportunities in the workplace.

■ Ask the children if they know what you call a person who designs houses and other buildings and discuss what an architect's job entails.

■ Invite the children over to the construction area, show them your half-built model and explain that the architect that started the job cannot finish it so they will have to.

■ Ask the children what they think the building is going to be and invite them to talk about the model they are going to construct.

■ Provide a range of construction equipment, such as DUPLO, LEGO, Mobilo, Sticklebricks or solid wooden blocks, for the children to use.

■ Include textured materials for the children to add to their constructions, such as carpet squares, corrugated cardboard, pie tins, egg-boxes and baskets. Discuss how these items feel and what they could be used for.

■ Encourage the children to add small-world people and animals to complete their constructions.

■ Give younger children more guidance about what kind of models to build, suggesting houses, hotels, farms, gardens, space stations, swimming-pools and zoos.

■ Allow older children to make their own designs from conception, through planning, to their final buildings.

More ideas
■ Gather empty boxes, for example, small washing-machine tablet boxes, shoeboxes and big fruit boxes for the children to construct with.

■ Let the children use construction kits to make a whole town for the small-world people and animals.

Home links
Ask parents and carers to show the children different types of building bricks and other building materials the next time they visit a DIY store.

Other curriculum areas
MD Encourage the children to make patterns using different-coloured bricks as they build their models.

KUW Show the children pictures of some famous buildings to copy, such as the Eiffel Tower, Taj Mahal, Great Wall of China and so on.

Stepping Stone
Begin to construct, stacking blocks vertically and horizontally and making enclosures and creating spaces.

Early Learning Goal
Explore colour, texture, shape, form and space in two or three dimensions.

Group size
Four to six children.

What you need
Books or posters about the jobs that people do; construction kits such as DUPLO, LEGO, Mobilo and Sticklebricks; solid wooden blocks; carpet squares; corrugated cardboard; foil pie tins; egg-boxes; baskets; small-world people and animals.

Preparation
Clear a large enough carpeted space for a small group to work comfortably. Before the children arrive use the equipment to begin a structure to encourage the children's imagination or for them to add to when they arrive.

Changing colours

Early Learning Goal
Explore colour, texture, shape, form and space in two or three dimensions.

Group size
Four to six children.

What you need
Paper plates; poster paints in blue, red and yellow; cling film; cartridge paper; squirt and spray canisters; strips of crêpe paper in vibrant colours measuring 15cm x 1cm.

Preparation
Prepare a paper plate for each child with a blob of each of the paints, making sure that they are not touching. Cover the plates with the paint on them with cling film.

Home links
Encourage parents and carers to let their children draw on sheets of kitchen roll with thick water-based marker pens and then to spray water lightly on top and observe the colours bleeding.

What to do
■ Give each child a plate and let them mix the colours by moving a finger gently across the top of the cling film.
■ Invite the children to talk about what they can see as they mix the paints. Can they see any new colours?
■ When they have finished mixing the colours, pull off the cling film and leave the plates to dry.
■ Continue exploring colour mixing by giving each child a large sheet of cartridge paper and asking the children to scatter strips of crêpe paper over it.

■ Invite the children to use the plant-spray canisters to lightly squirt water on top of the strips of crêpe paper. Observe the colours bleeding from the tissue paper on to the cartridge paper.
■ Draw the children's attention to areas where the colours have mixed. Ask the children what colour they can see where the yellow and blue have mixed, or where the yellow and red have mixed, and so on.
■ Use this activity as a stimulus for the children to start mixing their own colours when they are painting.
■ Talk about the names of the primary colours and how they can be mixed together to make new colours.
■ With younger children point out where the colours have mixed in their work and tell them the name of the new colour they have made.
■ Encourage older children to make a colour chart with the information they have learned about colour mixing.

More ideas
■ Give each child an unused paper filter for a coffee machine and encourage the children to make a design on it with vibrant water-based marker pens. Spray water on to the filter and watch the colours mix.
■ Secure a length of lining paper to an outdoor fence or wall. Fill several plant spray bottles with different colours of thinned, ready-mixed water-based paint and let the children spray the paper, encouraging them to allow the paints to mix as they run down. Discuss the changes and new colours that are formed when the paints mix.

Other curriculum areas
PSED Look at the use of colour and paint-mixing during the festival of Holi. Dip teabags in ready-mixed paint and drop them on to a sheet of cartridge paper to create an interesting effect.

CLL Place pieces of coloured Cellophane over the pages of a book so that the children can change the colours of the illustrations.

Space collages

What to do

■ Discuss the pictures in the information books with the children. Talk about what the surfaces of the planets look like and look at the bumps, craters, rocks and so on that can be seen.

■ Place the large piece of card flat on a table-top and invite the children to glue some of the small items on to the card using PVA glue. Fill small gaps with sand, lentils, pasta, rice and so on.

■ Leave the glue to dry. Mix gold, silver or bronze powder paint with PVA glue and let the children apply a coat of this mixture, using large household paintbrushes, to cover the card and the items glued to it.

■ When this is dry, encourage the children to add colour by applying crayons, pastels, pencils and chalks.

■ Let the children colour and cut out the space creatures from the photocopiable sheet so that they can play with them on their 'planets'.

■ As an alternative, instead of using the mixture of paint and glue, allow the children to cover their surface with tin foil. Invite them to apply a mixture of black paint and washing-up liquid to give an interesting finish to the planets.

■ With younger children colour and cut out the space creatures from the photocopiable sheet so that they are ready to play with.

■ Challenge older children to use craft materials to make additional features, such as space rockets, aliens, flags, space buggies and so on.

Other curriculum areas

CLL Paint the aliens from the photocopiable sheet and glue collage materials on top. Make alliterative names for the aliens that are created, such as 'Amy the Alien'.

PSED Invite the children to select from a range of media to create aliens, moon buggies or planets. Encourage the children to clear everything away when they have finished their creations.

More ideas

■ Make collages by cutting and tearing shapes and gluing them on to paper. The children can draw in details using crayons.

■ Use marbling inks with collage materials stuck on top with PVA glue to make planets.

Home links
Encourage parents and carers to take their children outdoors at night to look at the stars.

Musical shakers

Stepping Stone
Make constructions, collages, paintings, drawings and dances.

Early Learning Goal
Explore colour, texture, shape, form and space in two or three dimensions.

Group size
Four to six children.

What you need
The photocopiable sheet 'Gloop and papier mâché' on page 80; ingredients for one of the papier-mâché recipes; funnels; rice; lentils; dried peas; dry sand; small bells; balloons; musical shakers; empty flowerpots; newspaper; paint; collage materials; PVA glue.

Preparation
Make papier-mâché paste using one of the recipes on the photocopiable sheet.

Home links
Ask parents and carers to save old newspapers for creative activities. Place a box at the entrance for donations.

What to do
■ Explain to the children that they are going to be making their own musical shakers.

■ Listen to some of the manufactured shakers you have in your group. Ask the children to guess what is inside them. Encourage the children to suggest items that they could place inside their instruments.

■ Supervise the children as they use a funnel to place pieces of rice, lentils, dried peas, dry sand or small bells into a balloon. An adult should blow up each balloon and tie a knot in it.

■ Place the balloons in flowerpots with about two-thirds sticking out, to make it easier for the children to work with the papier mâché.

■ Demonstrate to the children how to dip newspaper strips into the paste, skim off the excess with your fingers, and lay the strips on the balloon. Apply about three or four layers, then turn the balloon the other way round to cover it.

■ Leave to dry. When completely dry, burst the balloons with a needle.

■ Allow the children to decorate their shakers with paint, tissue shapes and other collage materials.

■ Help younger children to apply the strips of newspaper so that the task does not become tedious.

■ Invite older children to make repeated patterns on their shakers using paints, thick markers or collage materials.

More ideas
■ Make guitars from empty tissue boxes and elastic bands.

■ Punch holes around the edge of a paper plate and attach small bells to make a tambourine.

Other curriculum areas
PSED Talk about recycling paper and other materials. Discuss why this is a good idea. Make a collage using recycled paper and card.

PD Use the finished instruments to make music for other children in the group to move and dance to.

Kitchen printing

What to do

■ Gather the children round the table you are going to be working at and draw their attention to the items gathered in the basket or plastic basin.

■ Ask the children to name and guess what some of the different items are used for.

■ Give each child a large piece of craft paper. One at a time, invite the children to select an item from the basket and to dip the end of the object into one of the containers of paint.

■ Let the children enjoy building up their creations using the different kitchen items.

■ Draw the children's attention to some of the patterns that they are creating by printing on to the paper.

■ Demonstrate to younger children how some of the more unusual items should be handled.

■ Give older children small challenges to encourage them to use overlapping, fitting, in, out and so on, for example, 'Can you fit something inside that shape, Simon?' or 'Let's see if you can get those two to overlap on your paper, Gabriel'.

More ideas

■ Dip the wheels of toy cars and other vehicles in paint and 'drive' them across sheets of paper. Use different colours of paint and sizes of vehicle to create a tartan effect.

■ Make a collage using ripped or torn pieces of paper. Encourage the children to make the pieces touch and overlap. Extend this activity by inviting the children to cut out shapes for their collage that will fit into one another or cut strips to make a grid effect.

Other curriculum areas

MD Cut shapes from a range of textures that the children can use to make collages and develop their positional language as they place pieces.

PD Give the children instructions to move hoops, quoits, bands, mats and beanbags around using ideas that involve fitting, overlapping, in, and out.

Home links

Ask parents to donate old kitchen utensils that could be used for this activity.

Stepping Stone

Use ideas involving fitting, overlapping, in, out, enclosure, grids and sun-like shapes.

Early Learning Goal

Explore colour, texture, shape, form and space in two or three dimensions.

Group size

Up to ten children.

What you need

Empty, shallow, plastic food containers; various colours of ready-mixed poster paints; coloured craft paper; wide range of kitchen items, such as yoghurt pots, ice-cube trays, pastry cutters, spatulas, fish slices, forks, potato mashers, sieves, strainers, whisks, lids of jars, lids of fabric-softener containers, suitable fruit and vegetables, straws, eggcups, paper cups and so on.

Preparation

Place all the gathered items in a basket or plastic basin. Pour the different colours into separate shallow containers.

Sunflowers

Stepping Stone
Choose particular colours to use for a purpose.

Early Learning Goal
Explore colour, texture, shape, form and space in two or three dimensions.

Group size
Up to ten children.

What you need
A bunch of fresh flowers; self-drying modelling clay; circles of coloured tissue paper; viewfinder or magnifying glass; green drinking straws.

Home links
Hold an exhibition of the children's works of art and invite parents and carers to come and visit.

Other curriculum areas

MD Play colour-matching games.

PSED Talk about favourite colours for food, clothes, flowers, cars and so on.

What to do

■ Gather the children round the bunch of flowers and invite them to look at the flowers closely, using a viewfinder or magnifying glass. Talk about the colours and shapes that they can see.

■ Encourage them to smell and feel the different parts of the flowers, reminding the children to be careful as they touch them.

■ Invite the children to choose from the following different ways of recording what the flowers look like.

■ Let them choose particular colours from a range of mark-making implements, such as pencils, crayons, chalks or pens, to make detailed drawings of the flowers.

■ Ask the children to cut the green drinking straws in half. Give each child a lump of clay to place the cut straws in, like sunflower stems. Provide them with circles of tissue paper and encourage them to select the appropriate colours to glue on to the straws as sunflower heads.

■ Cut petals from different colours of felt and place them in a small box. Encourage the children to select the correct colours and arrange them to make a sunflower. Add stems and leaves.

■ Provide younger children with a square of green card approximately 20cm by 20cm, turn it like a diamond shape and roll the East and West corners towards the centre to look like a bouquet. Allow the children to select the appropriate colours of tissue paper to glue at the North corner to look like a bouquet of sunflowers.

■ With older children gather a range of colours and textures of material that have been pre-cut into strips approximately 5cm by 2cm. After discussion about the colours of a sunflower, allow the children to select several pieces of material in appropriate colours for the flowers and encourage them to lay them in a pile on top of one another. Tie the pile in the centre tightly with a pipe-cleaner to make a flower head. Use these to make a sunflower collage.

More ideas

■ Look at the website www.vangoghgallery.com/misc/sunflowers.htm with the children to see how Van Gogh depicted sunflowers in several different paintings.

■ Invite the children to carefully mix their own shades of paint to make their own paintings of sunflowers.

Play-dough creatures

What to do

■ Draw the children's attention to some of the photographs in the books and posters. Talk about the features of the various animals. Ask questions that will help focus their observations, for example, do all the animals have tails, which have wings and so on.

■ Focus on the texture of each of the animals. Use adjectives such as 'soft', 'hard', 'prickly', 'smooth', 'spiky', 'furry', 'shiny', 'rough', 'flat', 'lumpy', 'stretchy', 'crinkly', 'jagged', 'fluffy' and 'bumpy'.

■ Then give each child some of the play dough to use.

■ Put out copies of the photocopiable sheet 'Play-dough shapes' for the children to use as reference. Invite them to take their balls of dough and explain that you want them to try to make a model of one of the animals that they can see in the photographs.

■ Let the children make the basic body shapes then create textures by adding raisins and other dried fruit, desiccated coconut, chocolate chips, sand, woodchips, glitter, sequins, lentils, pasta pieces, rice, pipe-cleaners and feathers.

■ Demonstrate to younger children how to make different shapes with the dough, for example, rolling a round ball or a long worm shape. Let them use the photocopiable sheet for guidance.

■ Invite older children to make up names for the creatures that they have created.

Home links

Place some play dough in a zip-lock bag for children to take and use at home. Enclose a recipe sheet so that parents and carers can make their own if they wish to do so.

More ideas

■ Show the children how to use a garlic press, sieve, shells, nuts and bolts, keys, biscuit cutters, scraps of net curtain, corrugated card, plastic shapes, LEGO pieces, Sticklebricks and so on to create different textures in the play dough.

■ Provide wet and dry sand for the children to play with. Let them try to create different textures in the sand using various implements.

Other curriculum areas

MD Follow a recipe to make bread dough with the children. Bake some bread rolls and enjoy creating different textures on top before eating them.

PD Experiment to make different textures of whipped pudding, mashed potatoes or play dough. Allow the children to take turns to manipulate the different textures and consistencies.

Creative development

Texture paintings

Stepping Stone
Experiment to create different textures.

Early Learning Goal
Explore colour, texture, shape, form and space in two or three dimensions.

Group size
Up to ten children.

What you need
The photocopiable sheets 'Paint recipes' and 'Make your mark' on pages 82 and 85; ingredients for the paint recipes; combs; hairbrushes; toothbrushes; bottle brushes; plastic forks; lolly sticks; scrubbing brushes; grout applicators; poster paints; powder paints; large sheets of paper; paper plates; pieces of different-textured paper; plastic; fabric.

Preparation
Following the recipes on the photocopiable sheet on page 82, prepare some of the paint mixtures.

Home links
Create a 'recipe book' that carers can use to make the different types of paint at home to use with their children.

What to do
■ Mix one of the paints described on the photocopiable sheet to a reasonably thick consistency and invite the children to place large blobs of it on to a sheet of paper.

■ Give the children an opportunity to spread the paint using combs of various thicknesses, grout applicators and hairbrushes to 'comb' through it. Encourage them to use the other items listed to make different marks and movements on the paper.

■ Talk about the different marks and movements that they are creating and encourage them to do the same with some of the different-textured paints.

■ Provide the children with other surfaces to use the paint on, for example, corrugated card, sandpaper, embossed wallpaper, plastic, fabric and so on.

■ Allow the children to choose their favourite type of paint and their favourite mark maker to create a design on a paper plate that can then be made into a group display.

■ Hand out copies of the photocopiable sheet 'Make your mark' and encourage the children to complete the squares of different marks on the sheet and create their own patterns in the last box. Allow them to colour their creations if they choose to.

■ Limit the choice of types of applicators and surfaces until younger children become comfortable in using them.

■ Challenge older children to make specific marks on the paper, for example, solid lines, thick and thin lines, spirals, spots, ripples, waves, curls, dots, zigzags and so on.

Other curriculum areas
CLL Write out the instructions for making the paint recipes and annotate with drawings. Allow the children to follow the recipes to make the paint mixtures.

KUW Look at and feel the different textures of wall coverings in the local environment, such as brick walls, painted walls, papered walls, glass walls and so on.

More ideas
■ Add spoonfuls of sawdust, sand or crushed breakfast cereal to any liquid paint for a grainy, bumpy texture.

■ Use different everyday items for making a variety of marks on paper with paint, for example, empty roll-on deodorant bottles, empty shoe-polish applicators and empty plastic sauce bottles.

Chinese dragons

What to do

◼ Look at some pictures of dragons from Chinese New Year celebrations. If you have Internet access, have a look at the website www.chinatown-online.org.uk/celebrations.html

◼ Encourage the children to add coloured poster paint of their choice to the cooled paint mixture that you have made in advance.

◼ Invite the children to apply a layer of this thick mixture with a plastic knife to three compartments of an upturned egg-box, to empty cheese-triangle boxes, or to any other appropriately shaped cardboard containers, to form a dragon.

◼ Encourage the children to decorate their dragons by sticking collage materials to the damp mixture. Invite them to select materials independently choosing from sequins, scrunched-up chocolate wrappers, buttons, pebbles, feathers, strips of crêpe paper and so on.

◼ When the paint mixture is dry, the collage materials will stick firmly to it without using any adhesive.

◼ Add long strips of material to the back section to form a body.

◼ Invite the children to make a table-top display of their finished dragons for everyone to see.

◼ Help younger children to apply the thick mixture of paint to the empty containers.

◼ Show older children how to stick short garden canes to the small dragons to create puppets.

More ideas

◼ Experiment with a range of techniques to see which works best on the different containers available.

◼ Try mixing paint with PVA glue, flour, washing-up liquid and non-fungicidal wallpaper paste.

Other curriculum areas

MD Work on a large scale by inviting the children to create a dragon's head using a range of recyclable and craft materials. Show them how to use an empty crisp box as a base and add cheese-triangle boxes, egg-boxes, cardboard tubes, foil paper, Cellophane, recycled pots, tissue paper, crêpe paper and so on. Encourage the children to talk about the shapes that they are using.

PSED Make Chinese dragons from paper plates, attaching strips of material or crêpe paper as bodies. Allow the children to dance to Chinese music with the dragons that they have made.

Hessian art

Stepping Stone
Work creatively on a large or small scale.

Early Learning Goal
Explore colour, texture, shape, form and space in two or three dimensions.

Group size
Four to six children.

What you need
Hessian sack (local Chinese or Indian restaurants may have old rice sacks available); strips of fabric, ribbon, wool; crêpe paper; rope; leaves; sheep's wool; feathers; long grasses; magnifying glass.

Home links
Share ideas with parents and carers to allow their children to take part in outdoor art at home, such as painting with water on a warm day, using squirt and spray bottles, buckets of water, large paintbrushes and paint rollers to play with on a slabbed area or on a wall.

What to do

■ Explain to the children that fabrics are made up of threads. Look at various fabrics using a magnifying glass to see all the different threads.
■ Give the children scraps of material that have frayed edges and let them pull on the loose threads. Discuss what happens to the materials.
■ Give each child a square of hessian about 25cm by 25 cm. Ask them to pull out one thread, then another.
■ Tell them to pull out three threads from each of the four edges to create a fringe. Encourage them to pull out others so that there are gaps in their square.
■ Starting from one end, encourage the children to weave strips of fabric, ribbon, wool, crêpe paper, rope, leaves, sheep's wool, feathers or long grasses through their squares of material.
■ Encourage them to continue weaving until all the gaps are filled up.
■ Display the finished creations on the wall or use them as placemats.
■ Start off the weaving for younger children as this is the most difficult part of the process.
■ With older children introduce the concept of making a pattern in the hessian as they weave.

More ideas

■ Make a nature collage using a piece of bark or plywood as a base. Glue on dried weeds, wood shavings, sawdust, pine cones, seed pods, pine needles, shells from nuts, leaves, pebbles, sand and so on.
■ Look at books or search the Internet to look at the work of Andy Goldsworthy, a British environmental artist who uses natural materials, often on a large scale.

Other curriculum areas

KUW Use similar materials in large-scale weaving. Use a fence or drape a piece of garden netting and allow the children to explore their local environment for materials to weave with, including ribbon, wool, leaves, feathers, beads, twigs, bark, netting, long grasses and so on.

PD Use empty plastic fruit baskets for weaving similar materials as those described above.

Use the ideas in this chapter to build on the children's natural sense of rhythm and awareness of sound. The activities describe ways in which the children can make sounds and music as well as providing opportunities for them to move to music.

Karaoke kids

What to do

■ Ask the children to name their favourite songs and allow the group to sing each one in turn either accompanying them on a piano or playing a song tape.

■ Give the children pretend microphones to sing into. These could be wooden spoons, hairbrushes and so on.

■ Observe the children singing and look out for those who do not open their mouths or who keep them open without mouthing words, and be prepared to provide support where necessary.

■ Hold these 'karaoke' sessions within the group on a regular basis, enjoying a range of songs that are familiar to the children.

■ With younger children sing along with all the songs yourself, modelling the use of the 'microphone'. Invite the children to join in when they are ready. Some children might initially just mime along to a tape or the other children singing. Promote their confidence by singing some question-and-answer songs that include repetitive phrases.

■ With older children allow smaller groups, or individuals, to perform their favourite song for the other children.

More ideas

■ Nominate a nursery rhyme or song of the day. Sing it at snack time, tidy-up time or as the children get ready to go home and theme your role-play area to suit the rhyme.

■ Sing well-known songs, leaving out some of the words for the children to contribute.

Other curriculum areas

PSED Encourage the children to support each other in their singing and join in praise and appreciation for those who have sung well.

MD Include counting songs or rhymes in the sessions.

CLL Introduce the concept of rhyming by asking the children 'Which words sound the same?' as you sing.

Stepping Stone
Join in favourite songs.

Early Learning Goal
Recognise and explore how sounds can be changed, sing simple songs from memory, recognise repeated sounds and sound patterns and match movements to music.

■

Group size
Up to 20 children.

■

What you need
Tape recorder or CD player; tapes or CDs of children's songs, or a piano; wooden spoons, hairbrushes or similar.

Home links
Encourage parents and carers to share songs that the children enjoy at home and incorporate these into the group's singing sessions. Ask adults to identify which song their child enjoys the most and make a display chart showing the overall favourite song.

Shake, rattle and tap

Stepping Stone
Show an interest in the way musical instruments sound.

Early Learning Goal
Recognise and explore how sounds can be changed, sing simple songs from memory, recognise repeated sounds and sound patterns and match movements to music.

Group size
Four to six children.

What you need
A selection of instruments, such as woodblocks, tambourines, triangles, shakers and chime bars; tape recorder or CD player; tapes or CDs.

Home links
Ask parents and carers to make shakers with their children at home by filling small, plastic bottles with dried peas or rice. These can be used to shake out a beat when the children sing or listen to music at home.

What to do
■ Introduce a sign for 'stop playing', this could be a hand signal, a picture on card, a whistle blast and so on.
■ Allow the children to have a free-play session with the instruments and practise using the stop signal.
■ Play some music with a strong, simple beat on tape or CD and encourage the children to join in with their instruments.
■ After exploring the instruments, ask the children to decide which ones make a loud sound and which make a quiet sound.
■ Play all the quiet sounding instruments together, then play all the loud sounding ones together. Ask the children which they prefer.
■ Ask the children to investigate whether they can make a quiet instrument sound louder and vice versa. How did they achieve this? Discuss what they find.
■ Let younger children each choose an instrument and adapt the song 'Here We Go Round the Mulberry Bush' to 'This is the way Joe beats the drum' and so on, encouraging the named child to play along.
■ With instruments grouped into loud and quiet, encourage older children to suggest ideas for what each instrument sounds like, for example, a chime bar could be a clock striking.

More ideas
■ Draw symbols to represent shaking, tapping or beating and allocate the instruments. Invite the children to play their instrument when you hold up the corresponding symbol.
■ Form a circle and ask one child to sit in the middle and to cover their eyes. Ask another child to play an instrument and see if the child in the centre can guess the instrument correctly. Let each child have a turn.

Other curriculum areas
PD Form a marching band. Appoint a leader and ask the children to play as they march, keeping to the beat of their feet. As they progress, the leader could play their instrument held high or low, indicating that the other children should play loudly or quietly.

CLL Discuss opposites while exploring the instruments, for example, loud and quiet, fast and slow, and high and low. Extend to other vocabulary, such as up and down, in and out, and so on.

Creative development

Body rhythm

What to do

▪ Tell the children that you are going to play some different pieces of music. Try to play some reggae, some classical and some pop music.

▪ Discuss the beat, rhythm and speed of the music. Ask the children if they can think of appropriate movements which match the music.

▪ Play the music again and give the children time to explore different movements while they listen to it.

▪ Offer the children scarves or ribbons to accompany their movements.

▪ Ask the children to find one movement that they feel fits each particular piece of music best, making sure they choose a different one for each piece. For example, twirling slowly to a classical piece, skipping to rock and roll and bending their knees to reggae.

▪ Let the children watch each other to share ideas.

▪ Ask the children to try to put the three movements together to form a short sequence.

▪ For younger children model the kind of movements that are appropriate to the different pieces of music. Hold the hands of children who require support.

▪ With older children, nominate a leader to initiate movements for the other children to follow. Repeat the movements in a four or eight pattern to fit in with the music and ensure that everyone gets a chance to lead.

More ideas

▪ Specify a part of the body that will move to a beat, and how it will move, such as 'shrugging shoulders'. Ask the children to follow the instructions as you beat a drum.

▪ Select a piece of music that has distinct high and low sections. Ask the children to stretch up high when the music is high and crouch down low when the music is low.

Stepping Stone
Respond to sound with body movement.

Early Learning Goal
Recognise and explore how sounds can be changed, sing simple songs from memory, recognise repeated sounds and sound patterns and match movements to music.

▪

Group size
Up to ten children.

▪

What you need
Tape recorder or CD player; tapes or CDs of various types of music; scarves or ribbons.

Other curriculum areas

MD Make up a short sequence of movements with the children, which will be completed in time to your chosen music. This could be jumping, stretching, then clapping, with each of the movements to be repeated four times.

KUW Explore a range of music from different cultures.

Home links
Send home copies of the photocopiable sheet 'I like to... to music' on page 86 and ask parents and carers to discuss and complete the sheet with their children. Ask them to return the completed sheets to you and talk about what the children did.

Mood music

Early Learning Goal
Recognise and explore how sounds can be changed, sing simple songs from memory, recognise repeated sounds and sound patterns and match movements to music.

Group size
Up to ten children.

What you need
A tape recorder or CD player; music on tape or CD that represents something with which the children are familiar, for example, 'Aquarium' in *Carnival of the Animals* by Saint-Saëns.

Home links
Provide a list of suitable classical or multicultural pieces of music that parents and carers can share with their children. If you have tapes or CDs available, you could set up a lending library.

What to do
■ Ask the children to close their eyes while you play them the music you have chosen.
■ Invite the children to tell you what the music made them think about or how it made them feel. Suggest words to them, such as 'lively', 'busy' and so on.
■ Tell the children the name of the piece of music and what it was about – for example, the title 'Aquarium' suggests the sea and fish swimming in it.
■ Listen to the piece of music again, pointing out to the children which sounds make you think of waves and so on.
■ After discussion play the music again, this time asking the children to think of suitable movements to accompany it, such as weaving across the floor like a fish swimming through water.
■ Encourage the children to develop their own movement and to build up an 'underwater scene' to accompany the piece of music, with each child representing different sea creatures.
■ With younger children model appropriate movements. Hold the hands of children who require direct support.
■ Allow older children to lead the group in moving to the music, encouraging other children to follow the leader's ideas.

More ideas
■ Play several different pieces of music from *Carnival of the Animals* so that the children can compare, contrast and explore different kinds of movement to represent the different animals.
■ Play appropriate music for the conga dance and form a chain with the children, moving around the room in time to the music – one, two, three, kick and so on. Start slowly without the music then once the children have grasped the idea, add sound.

Other curriculum areas
CLL Read *Carnival of the Animals* illustrated by Sue Williams, commentary by Barrie Carson Turner (Henry Holt). Use the book as a basis for discussion, before listening and moving to the music.

PSED Show the children pictures of dancers from different cultures, or even invite a local group to visit. Let the children see their costumes, listen to the music and watch their movements. Encourage them to join in, imitating what they have seen.

Sing in a ring

Early Learning Goal
Recognise and explore how sounds can be changed, sing simple songs from memory, recognise repeated sounds and sound patterns and match movements to music.

Group size
Up to 20 children.

What you need
The photocopiable sheet 'Round the zoo' on page 87.

What to do

■ Sing through the first few verses of 'Round the zoo' several times, then ask the children to join in line by line.

■ Once they are familiar with these verses of the song, ask the children to form a big circle. Show them what the actions are for each part of the song and give them an opportunity to practise each action.

■ Now sing through the song together, doing the actions. Repeat this several times giving different children the roles involved. Continue through all the verses.

■ Encourage younger children to join in with the actions and repeated lines to begin with or allow them to simply watch the other children at first.

■ Give older children an instrument that they can use to add sound effects, such as castanets for the zebras hooves galloping.

More ideas

■ Share some other familiar songs and ring games, such as 'The Farmer's in the Dell', 'In and Out the Dusty Bluebells', 'Here We Go Round the Mulberry Bush' and 'The Hokey Cokey'.

■ Sing 'One Finger, One Thumb, Keep Moving' and model the actions, encouraging the children to join in.

Home links
Tell parents and carers which songs and games you are singing with the children and ask them to practise at home. Suggest that they share simple songs, such as 'If You're Happy and You Know It' (Traditional).

Other curriculum areas

CLL Talk about the animals that you would find in a zoo. Read *Giraffes Can't Dance* by Giles Andreae (Orchard Books) with the children and discuss Gerald's feelings in the story.

PD To the tune of 'She'll Be Coming Round the Mountain' (Traditional), sing:

We can all skip round together, here we go (x2)
We can all skip round together in any kind of weather
We can all skip round together, here we go.

Invite the children to stand in a circle and move around as they sing, doing the action. Add other verses, for example, with 'hop', 'crawl' and so on.

Creative development

Community singing

What to do

■ Practise between four and six songs until the children are confident in singing them. For a 'Summer holidays' theme you could choose songs such as 'The Sun Has Got His Hat on', 'Oh I Do Like to Be Beside the Seaside' (Traditional) and so on.

■ Tell the children they are going to sing the songs at a 'concert'.

■ Ensure that all the children know which song is linked to which picture so that you can hold up the correct picture when you want them to sing the corresponding song. Keep the order the same through the practices and the actual performance.

■ For the performance the children could wear shorts and T-shirts and have props for each song, such as a hat for 'The Sun Has Got His Hat on'.

■ Send out invitations stating date, time and venue of your sing-along and include reply slips so that you know how many visitors to expect.

■ On the day, seat the children so they are comfortable and can all be seen by the visitors. Enjoy your performance!

■ Give younger children a simple role, such as performing actions for the songs.

■ Suggest that older children have a more prominent role, perhaps participating in a duet or performing a solo.

More ideas

■ Choose from themes such as Christmas or Hanukkah. Ask an adult to provide a narrative between songs to link them.

■ Show the children part of a singing video or television programme such as 'The Singing Kettle' or 'Barney' and learn the songs together.

Home links
Invite parents and carers to the sing-along and give them a copy of the song sheet so they can practise the songs at home with their children.

Other curriculum areas

KUW Introduce multicultural celebrations and, to the tune of 'Frère Jacques' (Traditional), sing:
Divali's coming (x2), Festival of light (x2)
Paint rangoli patterns (x2), Celebrate all night (x2).

MD Make ten green paper bottles and number them from 1 to 10. Count them with the children, modelling the numeral. Sing 'Ten Green Bottles' removing one each time until there are none left.

Sing as we go

What to do

▪ Make up simple songs to accompany daily routines, for example, to the tune of 'Here We Go Round the Mulberry Bush' (Traditional):

This is the way we wash our hands, wash our hands, wash our hands, this is the way we wash our hands before we have our snack.

▪ As the children arrive and leave the group, sing the song, encouraging them to join in, for example, to the tune of 'There's a Hole in My Bucket' (Traditional):

Well, hello there, dear Cameron, (x3)
Well, hello there dear Cameron, how are you today?

▪ Model spontaneously creating songs during activities, for example, to the tune of 'The Wheels on the Bus' (Traditional):

Gabriel's jumping up and down, (x3)
Gabriel's jumping up and down, on the trampoline this morning.

▪ Suggest ideas or a structure for simple songs related to what younger children are doing and use tunes that the children know well. Don't worry about using too many words, just hum tunes.

▪ Ask older children to make up a song concerning their own actions and encourage independent choices.

More ideas

▪ When the children are using percussion instruments, sing this song and encourage the children to suggest words:

Come on let's ___, ___, ___ the bells.
Come on let's ___, ___, ___ the drums.

▪ Read Cows in the Kitchen by John Smith (Penguin) to the tune of 'Skip, Skip, Skip to My Lou' (Traditional) and encourage the children to suggest verses that are relevant to them, such as 'Sam's at the water tray, splash, splash, splash! (x3) On a bright and sunny Monday'.

Other curriculum areas

PSED During circle time, nominate each child in turn and ask the other children to think of something that the child is good at. To the tune of 'Pop Goes the Weasel' (Traditional), sing:

I know a boy/girl whose name is Kwok-Li
Kwok-Li is my friend
Kwok-Li is good at hopping around
My song is at an end.

CLL Support the children in thinking of words that begin with the same sound as their name, and string them together to the tune of 'Jelly on the Plate' (Traditional). Nonsense words are fine!

Tap to the beat

Stepping Stone
Tap out simple repeated rhythms and make some up.

Early Learning Goal
Recognise and explore how sounds can be changed, sing simple songs from memory, recognise repeated sounds and sound patterns and match movements to music.

Group size
Up to ten children.

What you need
Four or five pieces each of red, orange, blue and yellow card.

What to do
■ Sit in a circle and clap steadily together. If any of the children claps indiscriminately, stop and get everyone back in unison.
■ Say different colour names together and decide how many sounds they have, for example, red has one, yellow has two, and so on.
■ Explain that for each sound in the colour name you will give a clap – one clap for red, two for yellow, and so on. Practise this.

■ Show the children the coloured pieces of card and discuss how many claps you would give for each colour of card, for example, blue and red one clap each, yellow and orange two claps each, and so on.
■ Hold different cards up in a sequence and clap the rhythm that they make, without saying the colour names, for example, 'blue, yellow, blue, yellow' is 'clap, clap-clap, clap, clap-clap'.

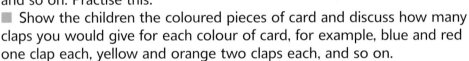

■ Let each child make a sequence and invite the other children to clap it out together.
■ Encourage younger children to say the colours shown in sequence, so that they can hear the rhythm of the words. Gently guide the hands of any children who cannot find the rhythm.
■ Clap out a rhythm then ask older children to arrange the colour cards to show what the sequence was. Gradually make the sequences longer.

Home links
Suggest that parents and carers sing simple nursery rhymes with their children, clapping out the beat as they sing.

Other curriculum areas
PD Help children to each find their own pulse as they sit at rest (try the neck or wrist) and ask them to say 'beat' in time with their pulse. Walk briskly round the room and then ask them to check their pulses again. Finally, jog around the room for a minute and check the pulses again. Ask the children what they notice. They should be saying 'beat' more quickly. Discuss why this happens.

KUW Investigate how cogs and wheels make the hands of a clock move and discuss what clocks do with the children. Make cardboard clock-faces with moving hands and sing 'Hickory Dickory Dock' (Traditional) together, asking the children to make a steady 'tick-tock' rhythm.

More ideas
■ Adapt the activity to clap the names of the children, then make sequences from them, saying the names as you clap, for example, 'Sam, Sam, Ra-vi, Sam'.
■ Use topic-related words in the same way. Draw pictures so the children can 'read' the rhythm to be clapped, for example, for a topic on 'The sea', clap the syllables for fish, light-house and oct-o-pus.
■ Introduce other methods of marking rhythm, such as stamping, clicking fingers and slapping thighs.

All change!

What to do

■ Sing a familiar song, such as 'Rock-a-bye Baby' (Traditional), through with the children.

■ Repeat the song, this time asking the children to sing it in a whispering voice and then again in a shouting voice.

■ Compare the different sounds that the children have made with their voices and discuss which volume is best for singing a lullaby.

■ Sing this song to the tune of 'In and Out the Dusty Bluebells' (Traditional), beginning with a normal singing voice then getting louder or quieter as required:

I can sing this very loudly (or quietly)
I can sing this very loudly (or quietly)
I CAN SING THIS VERY LOUDLY (or QUIETLY)
THIS TIME IS THE LOUDEST! (or QUIETEST)

■ Practise different voices with a simple question–answer exercise. Ask a child, 'Can you use your normal voice?' (speaking). They will answer 'I can use my normal voice' (speaking). Whisper, sing and shout a similar message and the child should answer in the same tone.

■ With younger children model the different voices and encourage them to join in. Say with them, 'Whisper, whisper, whisper' in a whisper, 'Speaking, speaking, speaking' spoken at normal volume, and 'Shouting, shouting, shouting' in a loud voice.

■ With older children decide upon signs which mean sing loudly (hands raised), quietly (hands lowered) and normally (hands clasped). As the children sing change your hand signals to notify the children to change their voices.

More ideas

■ Using non-tuned percussion instruments, explore with the children how different sounds can be made by beating an instrument hard and tapping it softly.

■ Explore changes in sound by playing a note on the piano loudly or quietly. Ask the children to pretend to be tortoises and say that if the sound is loud, they must hide in their shells (curl up, arms round head), if it is quiet they must come out and crawl around. Adapt this using low and high pitch.

Stepping Stone
Explore and learn how sounds can be changed.

Early Learning Goal
Recognise and explore how sounds can be changed, sing simple songs from memory, recognise repeated sounds and sound patterns and match movements to music.
■
Group size
Up to ten children.
■
What you need
Just the children.

Home links
Ask parents and carers to investigate environmental sounds with their children and to note down anywhere they observe changes, for example, when a tap is trickling, then is turned on full blast or the washing machine moves from the wash cycle to the spin cycle.

Other curriculum areas

PD Tiptoe around the room, walk round the room and then stamp round the room, listening to the difference in the noise made.

KUW Demonstrate how to use a tape recorder, CD player or television and explore how the volume control can make the sound louder or quieter.

Creative development

Shake it!

Stepping Stone
Explore and learn
how sounds can be
changed.

**Early Learning
Goal**
Recognise and
explore how sounds
can be changed, sing
simple songs from
memory, recognise
repeated sounds and
sound patterns and
match movements
to music.

Group size
Up to ten children.

What you need
Plastic cups; paper
bags; paper plates;
margarine tubs; sticky
tape; stapler; cling
film; dried pulses,
pasta and rice.

What to do
■ Tell the children that they are going to make shakers to use during their music or song time.
■ Let the children help you to fill separate plastic cups with dried kidney beans, rice, lentils and dried pasta shapes. Cover with cling film, secure with tape and label the contents of each cup.
■ Invite the children to compare the sounds of the shakers and discuss. Do the shakers all sound the same? What are the differences? Which filling makes the noisiest or quietest shaker?
■ Repeat the activity using the same contents, but this time fill different types of containers, such as cartons, margarine tubs, paper bags, paper plates stapled together, and so on. Discuss the differences in sound and ask questions as above.

■ Investigate what happens to the sound if you increase the amount of filling in a container, or if you combine different fillings in one container.
■ Allow younger children to enjoy playing with the shakers, encouraging them to find out which makes the loudest noise.
■ Challenge older children to find out which combination of container, contents and volume of contents makes the loudest or quietest sounds.

More ideas
■ Try using different types of beaters on an instrument. Explore what happens to the sound of a triangle being played, depending on where and how you hold it.
■ Give the children a tambourine and ask them to find four different ways to play it (shake, beat and so on). Observe the different sounds that are made.

Home links
Ask carers to fill glass beakers with differing amounts of water and to supervise their children in tapping them with a pencil. They can find out which beaker makes the lowest noise and which makes the highest.

Other curriculum areas
CLL Ask the children to predict what a cymbal will sound like. Strike it, then ask what they think will happen if you hold the edge of the cymbal when or just after it is struck.

KUW Invite a musician who plays a wind instrument or a guitar to come and play for the children. Make sure that they do not mind the children exploring their instrument under supervision. Investigate what happens when more strings are pressed or holes covered, while the instrument is played.

Creative development

Listen and move

What to do

◼ Tell the children to close their eyes and to listen to your chosen piece of music.

◼ Encourage them to say what the music made them think of and discuss their ideas. Ask them questions such as, 'What did you picture when your eyes were closed?' and 'Which sounds or part of the music made you feel like that?'.

◼ After the discussion, play the music again and invite the children to make movements to accompany what they have heard, saying, for example, 'Let's be fireworks zooming round the room, exploding!'.

◼ Make suggestions to younger children for movement ideas, for example, 'Can you march like a soldier?', 'Can you take steps like a huge giant?' and so on. Model the movements and take a child's hand to encourage them to participate.

◼ Encourage older children to respond spontaneously to what they hear, linking the music to role-play. For example, provide suitable dressing-up clothes and play *The Nutcracker Suite*.

More ideas

◼ Play sound effects as a stimulus for movements, such as hammering and drilling.

◼ Listen to 'Birdy Song' or 'Superman' by Black Lace (on *Black Lace's Greatest Ever Party Album*, Metro) and show the children the accompanying dances so that they can join in.

◼ Play waltz music and ask two adults to model a waltz. Invite children to choose soft toys to imitate the twirling paired dance, keeping in time to the music.

Other curriculum areas

CLL Think of different movement words, for example, 'crawling', 'shuffling' and so on. Ask the children to move in these ways to the music. Introduce new words to extend their vocabulary, such as 'slithering' and 'galloping'.

PD Encourage the children to move in a variety of ways to pieces of music. For example, say, 'You have to keep your knees on the ground when moving to this piece' to encourage them to focus on the movement of their heads and arms.

Stepping Stone
Imitate and create movement in response to music.

Early Learning Goal
Recognise and explore how sounds can be changed, sing simple songs from memory, recognise repeated sounds and sound patterns and match movements to music.

Group size
Up to ten children.

What you need
A tape recorder or CD player; tapes or CDs with appropriate music or sound effects.

Preparation
Select pieces of music that represent specific themes, for example, *American in Paris* by Gershwin (traffic), *The Nutcracker Suite* by Tchaikovsky (toys) or *Music for the Royal Fireworks* by Handel (fireworks).

Home links
Let parents and carers know about your work on music and movement, and encourage them to participate in paired movement or mirroring at home with their children, to their own choice of music.

Our box of songs

Stepping Stone
Begin to build a
repertoire of songs.

Early Learning Goal
Recognise and explore how sounds can be changed, sing simple songs from memory, recognise repeated sounds and sound patterns and match movements to music.

Group size
Up to ten children.

What you need
A large box; brightly coloured paper; small objects that link to various songs, such as a plastic spider for 'Little Miss Muffet' (Traditional).

Preparation
Cover the box with brightly coloured paper and label it 'Our song box'. Place the selected items inside the box.

Home links
Ask parents and carers to think of one song that their child does not know. Invite them to sing it to their child and to write it down if possible, so that you can introduce it to the group.

What to do

- Show the children the box and explain that each item inside represents a song that they know.
- Take out each item in turn, telling the children which song it represents.
- Sing each song in turn, showing the appropriate prop to the children.
- As you learn new songs add appropriate new objects to the box.
- During singing sessions allow children to pick an object from the box as a prompt to the whole group to sing the associated song.
- With younger children limit the number of objects in the box. Support the children in recognising which song is being represented by offering two suggestions for them to choose from.
- Encourage older children to link the object to the song unaided. Ask if there are any other songs that the object could represent, for example, the plastic spider could also be used for 'Incy Wincy Spider' (Traditional).

More ideas
- Make hand puppets to represent characters from songs, such as Little Bo Peep. Tell the children that when you show them the puppet they can sing the corresponding song.
- Draw some picture strips for songs that the children know. For example, for 'Jack and Jill' (Traditional), draw five sections showing: the two children; the hill; a bucket of water; Jack falling, and Jill falling. Display the different strips in turn, asking the children to sing the corresponding lines.

Other curriculum areas
MD Build up a bank of counting songs, such as 'Ten Green Bottles', 'This Old Man' and 'Once I Caught a Fish Alive' (Traditional).

CLL Try to find a song that begins with each letter of the alphabet: 'Away in a Manger', 'Baa Baa Black Sheep' (Traditional) and so on. If you cannot find one for a specific letter make up a new song to a well-known tune, incorporating the children's names or interests and teach this to the children.

Creative development

Sound story

What to do
■ Tell the children that you are going to read them a story. Ask them to identify where sounds could be added and what those sounds might be.
■ Read the story 'Jack and the Beanstalk' and discuss the children's ideas for suitable sounds. Prompt the children with questions such as, 'What sounds do you think the giant might make – loud or quiet?', 'Would the sound be repeated?' and 'Would it be fast or slow?'.
■ Display the percussion instruments and invite the children to explore the sounds they can produce.
■ Let the children choose which instrument they think makes the best sound to create the desired effect, for example, beating a drum to represent the giant.
■ Read the story through again and encourage the children to join in by playing their instruments at the appropriate points in the story.
■ Repeat the idea using any other stories.
■ Help younger children to find suitable instruments, and signal to them when they should begin and end playing.
■ Encourage older children to choose which sounds to reproduce and when to play them.

More ideas
■ Give the children copies of the photocopiable sheet on page 88 and invite them to link the items to the instruments that would make the most suitable sound.
■ Make your own instruments by using a cardboard box as a drum, stretching rubber bands around a shoebox and plucking it to make a guitar sound and using foil milk-bottle tops stuck on to paper plates to form a tambourine.

Other curriculum areas
KUW Gather instruments from other countries, such as castanets (Spain), panpipes (South America) and sitars (India), talk about where they come from and explore the sounds they make. Listen to recorded music that incorporates these sounds.
PSED Sit in a circle around a selection of instruments. Invite the children in turn to say, 'Today I feel...' and to choose an instrument that represents how they feel – for example, 'Today I feel happy' and the child shakes some sleigh bells.

Stepping Stone
Explore the different sounds of instruments.

Early Learning Goal
Recognise and explore how sounds can be changed, sing simple songs from memory, recognise repeated sounds and sound patterns and match movements to music.

Group size
Up to ten children.

What you need
A version of 'Jack and the Beanstalk' (Traditional); selection of percussion instruments.

Home links
Invite parents and carers to see the children add the instrumental effects to the story. Encourage them to use the correct names of the instruments with the children, 'You were playing the maracas' and to find out which instrument their child likes best.

Bounce to the beat

What to do

■ Ask the children to form a circle, facing inwards.

■ Invite one child to stand in the centre of the circle and to hold the ball.

■ Sing the song and ask the child in the centre to passe the ball to other children in the circle, bouncing it half-way between them on the word 'bouncing'.

■ The child receiving the ball passes it back to the middle child in the same way in the next line of the song. Continue around the circle passing the ball to each child in turn.

■ Repeat the game, giving different children a chance to be in the centre.

■ Support younger children by standing behind them with your hands over theirs and helping them to get the timing right. If the children find catching the ball too difficult, play the game by rolling the ball instead.

■ Challenge older children to throw the ball randomly to children in the circle, rather than following around in order. Try bouncing out on the word 'we' and making the return bounce on the word 'to'.

More ideas

■ Tap a steady beat on a tambourine and ask the children to walk in time. Slow the beat down or speed it up and tell the children to alter their pace accordingly.

■ Play a 'Follow-my-leader' game keeping in time to this song, to the tune of 'One Finger, One Thumb, Keep Moving' (Traditional): 'We're following on from the leader (x3), And keeping in time to the beat'.

Other curriculum areas

KUW Play rock and roll music and teach the children to 'hand jive' by patting thighs, bumping fists and so on. Look at photographs of people jiving from the 1950s and look at their clothes and hair. Ask children to find out if any of their grandparents remember the 1950s.

PD Form a circle with the children and play some ceilidh music. As a group, side-step in time to the music, first one way and then the other.

Imaginative play allows children to take on roles and act them out. The ideas in this chapter encourage the children to take control of their play and express themselves freely, the use of various resources helping to stimulate their imagination.

Pet carriers

What to do

■ Show the children the pet carrier and talk about its features, such as the handle, the size of the 'door' and air holes or slats, depending on the style.

■ Attach simple card handles to some empty boxes, then add a flap and make air holes using a screwdriver.

■ Encourage the children to place their 'pet' gently into one of the boxes to carry it to the vet's.

■ Discuss what the children could put in the carrier to make it more comfortable for their pet.

■ Let the children adopt the role of vet in turn, wearing the adult's shirt.

■ Participate in the play with younger children, either taking the role of the vet or modelling the use of the pet carrier.

■ Encourage older children to add dialogue to their play, explaining the problem to the vet and discussing what treatment is needed.

More ideas

■ Arrange for a vet to come to your setting and speak to the children about caring for animals.

■ Provide an empty box for the children to use with small-world toys. Give the children's imagination free rein, encouraging them to tell you what they are using the box as.

Other curriculum areas

CLL Read *Hairy Maclary's Rumpus at the Vet* by Lynley Dodd (Puffin – out of print) and encourage the children to join in the rhyming of the text.

KUW Talk about some of the more unusual pets that people have, such as spiders, snakes, frogs, rats and so on. Ask the children to think about how they could be transported, and use a variety of materials to make carriers.

Goals for the
**Foundation
Stage**

Stepping Stone
Pretend that one object represents another, especially when objects have characteristics in common.

Early Learning Goal
Use their imagination in art and design, music, dance, imaginative and role-play and stories.

Group size
Up to six children.

What you need
Empty boxes (such as from photocopier paper); strips of card; sticky tape; screwdriver (adult use); soft-toy pets; adult's white shirt; pet carrier.

Preparation
Ask the children if they have a pet that they have had to take to the vet's, and discuss how the pet was transported there. Invite each child to bring in a soft-toy pet.

Home links
Encourage parents and carers to take their children on any visits to the vet's. If they do not have a pet, ask them to cut out pictures of animals together for the children to use in their play.

Creative development

Off we go!

Stepping Stone
Pretend that one object represents another, especially when objects have characteristics in common.

Early Learning Goal
Use their imagination in art and design, music, dance, imaginative and role-play and stories.

Group size
Up to ten children.

What you need
Eleven small chairs set out in a row of pairs, with one in front; card; marker pens; small pieces of paper for tickets; hand bell.

Preparation
Practise singing 'The Wheels on the Bus' (Traditional) with the children. Make a bus-stop sign using the card and marker pens.

Home links
Ask parents and carers to donate old rail, bus, aeroplane or boat tickets or timetables for the children to use in their imaginative play.

What to do

■ Display the bus stop sign and encourage the children to queue by it.
■ Ask one child to be the driver and to hand out tickets as the children 'get on' the imaginary bus.
■ Once all the children are seated, invite them to sing 'The Wheels on the Bus'.
■ Make up some new verses as their journey progresses and they pretend to look out of the window. For example:

The lollipop lady says
Stop please, bus, (x3)
The lollipop lady says
Stop please, bus,
All day long.

■ Tell the children to put hands up or ring the hand bell when they want to get off the bus.
■ They could sing:

Kristian would like to get off the bus (x3)
Kristian would like to get off the bus
at the next stop please.

■ Take an active role in the bus journey with younger children, singing and helping to suggest new verses.
■ With older children introduce percussion instruments where appropriate to provide the noises of the bus, such as the windscreen wipers.

More ideas

■ Adapt this to any mode of transport and use corresponding songs, such as 'The Train Is A-coming' in *Apusskidu* by Beatrice Harrop (A & C Black).
■ Cover a large empty box with foil to create a rocket and sing songs about space travel together.

Other curriculum areas

MD Provide play money or counters for the children to pay their fares on the bus.

KUW Discuss air travel and introduce words such as 'pilot', 'air hostess', 'take-off' and 'landing'. Set out chairs with a central aisle, provide some props such as a pilot's cap, and encourage the children to incorporate the information discussed into a role-play.

Dance away

What to do

■ Give each child a ribbon-stick and ask them to find a space in the room. Discuss safe use of the ribbon-sticks.

■ Demonstrate to the children how to use the ribbon in a variety of ways, such as making large circular motions with your arm, small circular motions from the wrist or wave-effect motions by flicking the wrist rapidly up and down.

■ Discuss the different effect each of these methods has on the way the ribbons move.

■ Give the children time to try these movements and to experiment with others, taking care that they are not standing too closely together.

■ Now play your selected music and invite the children to incorporate the ribbon movements into a simple dance – tapping their feet from side to side, twirling, stretching and so on. Observe how well the children are incorporating the ribbons into their dance movements.

■ Guide younger children, by holding their hand, while they move their ribbons.

■ Encourage older children to create a sequence of four movements that can be repeated to each chorus of the music.

More ideas

■ Make up a simple dance to a popular song or tune. Practise the dance with the children, then let them try to repeat it independently.

■ Learn 'The Hokey Cokey' (Traditional) and demonstrate the actions.

Other curriculum areas

PSED Demonstrate how to set the table for snack or lunchtime, showing the children what should be at each place setting, over several sessions. Ask the children to set the table unaided the following week.

PD Show the children how to do up a zip, fasten buttons and so on, and encourage them to try these unaided.

Home links
Allow the children to take the ribbon-sticks home to explore their movements further and to demonstrate their new skills to their parents and carers.

A bag of props

Early Learning Goal
Use their imagination in art and design, music, dance, imaginative and role-play and stories.

Group size
Up to ten children.

What you need
A cloth sack; variety of objects, such as a wooden spoon, scarf, cardboard tube and so on.

Home links
Cut out cardboard hoops and send one home with each child. Ask parents and carers to write down all the suggestions that their child gives for what the hoop could be – a halo, a bangle and so on.

What to do

■ Gather the children together into a large circle and talk to them about pretend play.

■ Explain that sometimes we can use things in our play that we pretend are something else. For example, an old sheet or a towel could become a flying carpet, cloak or a tent.

■ Tell the children that you are going to pass around a bag containing lots of different items. Explain that they have to choose an item, then think of something else it could be used to represent.

■ Demonstrate by pulling a cardboard tube from the bag and saying it could be a telescope, a trumpet or a microphone.

■ Encourage the children to each take a turn.

■ With younger children provide contexts, for example, ask them what a wooden spoon could become that a fairy might use (a wand).

■ Encourage older children to mime what their object could represent and to see if the other children can guess what it is.

More ideas

■ Collect the inner tubes from long rolls of tin foil or cling film and use them to represent umbrellas. Cut out some large circles from blue paper as puddles on the ground. Play music such as 'Singing in the Rain' (Big Blue Dog Records) and let the children mime dancing in rainy weather.

■ Give children a large cardboard box and encourage them to think of this as a context for their play, such as a boat, car or spaceship.

Other curriculum areas

CLL Encourage the children to describe an object and how it is used without actually saying what the object is. From the descriptions, try to guess what the object in mind was.

CD Choose different-textured paper, materials and items such as leaves and twigs to represent other things on a large collage linked to your current theme. For example, use different-coloured and different-sized leaves to represent fish.

The hat factory

What to do

■ Read the rhyme 'Who will I be?' on the photocopiable sheet and talk about the different types of hats and people mentioned. Show the children examples of hats that you have available.

■ Ask the children to each think about just one character and to consider what sort of hat he or she might wear. Would the chosen character be friendly, scary, helpful or bossy? Would their hat be large, small, coloured, fancy or plain?

■ Show the children the craft materials and, through discussion, help them to create the basic shape for their character's hat.

■ Ask the children to think about which colours, paper or fabrics are suitable for the hat and allow them to decorate it as required.

■ With younger children provide a variety of basic hat shapes ready-made from card and invite them to select a suitable one for their chosen character and to decorate it accordingly.

■ Once the hats are completed, encourage older children to wear them and adopt the role of their chosen character, considering how they would move, speak and what they might do.

More ideas

■ Set up the role-play area as a pirate ship. Assist the children in creating 'treasures' for the role-play using recycled boxes and coloured foil paper, or pasta shapes threaded on to string and sprayed gold or silver.

■ Make animal masks with the children to use in a farm role-play activity.

Other curriculum areas

PSED Discuss birthdays and how it feels to give a gift to a friend and see their pleasure. Set up the role-play area for a birthday party and ask the children to make banners and cards and to wrap empty boxes as gifts.

PD Talk about sportsmen and women and events such as the Olympics. Make medals using card, gold paint, foil and ribbon. Hold mini sports events during session times and award each participant a medal.

Growing sunflowers

What to do

■ Read the story *Daisy's Giant Sunflower* and discuss how Daisy had to plant the seed in a suitable place and how it needed the sun and rainwater to grow.

■ Look at the sunflower seeds and let the children touch and hold them.

■ Ask the children to curl up into the smallest shape they can, on their knees, to represent a sunflower seed.

■ Explain that the rain has fallen and now the sun is shining. Ask the children to

think about beginning slowly to 'grow'. Suggest that at first they stretch up an elbow, then a forearm and hand. Repeat with the other arm.

■ Slowly begin to uncurl the head and straighten the back and neck upwards. Emphasise how slow and steady the movements should be.

■ Encourage the children to slowly kneel up off their heels and finally to stand on two feet, stretching on to tiptoe.

■ Practise this sequence several times.

■ Next, play the music and ask the children to repeat their sequence of movements as it plays.

■ Demonstrate the movements and sequence for younger children.

■ Encourage older children to rise up and begin to bend towards the card 'sun', following it as you move it 'across the sky'.

More ideas

■ Sing 'Mary, Mary, Quite Contrary' (Traditional) and talk about the flowers in her garden. Repeat the activity miming the flowers 'all in a row'.

■ Make up a sequence of movements to represent a chick hatching out of an egg.

Other curriculum areas

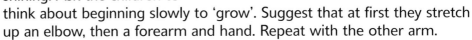
KUW Read *The Very Hungry Caterpillar* by Eric Carle (Hamish Hamilton). Discuss how caterpillars build a cocoon and transform into butterflies. Create a sequence of movements to represent the story and set it to appropriate music.

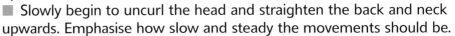
MD Teach the children the rhyme 'One, Two, Buckle My Shoe' (Traditional) and think of appropriate movements for the children to complete as they 'count.'

Creative development

Tell the story

What to do

■ Read out the rhyme on the photocopiable sheet and tell the children that you are going to put movements to each part of it.

■ Now, read the rhyme again, this time pausing to demonstrate each action suggested on the sheet.

■ Give the children plenty of opportunity to practise each of the different movements.

■ Read the rhyme through once again, this time with the children putting the actions into sequence to bring the story to life.

■ Participate in the actions with younger children to help them remember what to do.

■ Challenge older children to remember the movements without any prompting, as you read the rhyme aloud to them.

More ideas

■ Read *We're Going on a Bear Hunt* by Michael Rosen (Walker Books) and invite the children to join in with the repeated lines and the corresponding actions.

■ Teach the children the song and dance 'The Grand Old Duke of York' (Traditional), where they have to side-step between two rows of children with a partner, 'cast off', leading a row of children, and meet up with their partner again to form a bridge which the other children pass below.

Other curriculum areas

CLL Ask the children to suggest some movement words and make up short poems putting the words together. Include repetition, for example, 'Jump, jump, skip, hop, jump.' Repeat these over a few times, then encourage the children to put the actions for the rhyme together in sequence.

KUW Talk about the life cycle of frogs and, if possible, show the children tadpoles at different stages. Put together a sequence of actions that represent the different stages – spawn, swimming tadpole, tadpole with legs and tail creeping around, jumping frog.

Creative development

All about me

Stepping Stone
Enjoy stories based on themselves and people and places they know well.

Early Learning Goal
Use their imagination in art and design, music, dance, imaginative and role-play and stories.

Group size
Up to ten children.

What you need
Sheets of sugar paper; selection of photographs of each of the children; glue sticks; pens and pencils; scissors; stapler; sticky tape; photographs of yourself.

Preparation
Make an example of a story-book 'All about me' and include references to friends, holidays, my birthday, my house and so on. The book could start 'This is Wendy. She lives in Littlehill. She has two children called Katie and Andrew'. Keep each page simple, with a short sentence and linked picture or photograph.

What to do
Tell the children that you are going to read them a very special story and show them the book that you have made. Tell the story, showing them your pictures and photographs.

Note the reactions of the children as they realise that this book refers to people and places they recognise.

When you have read your story, tell the children that they are each going to make a book about themselves and their families.

Under adult supervision let the children plan each page of their books and draw pictures or stick in photographs. Encourage them to discuss the pictures and scribe a sentence for each one.

Read the books aloud for younger children at story time.

Encourage older children to 'read' the books to the others at story time, talking through each page.

More ideas
Make up stories involving people and places that the children know, incorporating an element of choice as to the direction that the story takes, for example, 'Paul went to the library or to the park?'.

Encourage paired storytelling, taking turns to say something that the children have done.

Other curriculum areas
KUW Provide opportunities for the children to use scissors, stapler, sticky tape and glue spreaders as they make their books.

MD Make a counting book with each child of the things they like. For example, 'Poppy's Favourite Toys' could have '1 doll's house', '2 puppets', '3 teddy bears' and so on. Cut pictures from catalogues or draw the corresponding number of items on each page.

Home links
Ask parents and carers to provide suitable photographs for their child to make a personal book.

The shoe shop

What to do

■ Ask the children to sit in a circle with their feet outstretched.

■ Go round the group and comment on the different shoes you can see. Point out what colour each pair is and how they fasten (for example, laces, buckles or Velcro).

■ Ask the children to think about when their shoes were bought. Where did they go? What did they have to do? How were their feet measured? Did they try on lots of pairs of shoes?

■ After the discussion, direct the children to the role-play area that you have created and encourage them to take the role of either the shop assistant or a customer in the shoe shop.

■ Demonstrate the kinds of questions they might ask, such as, 'Are you looking for summer shoes or boots?' and 'Do you have any shoes with Velcro fastening?'.

■ With younger children take on the role of the assistant yourself initially, measuring feet and fetching pairs of shoes.

■ Challenge older children by placing a photograph on each box of which shoes it should contain and asking them to put pairs of shoes into the correct one.

More ideas

■ Create a role-play of a florist's shop with pictures of flowers, ribbons and bows, silk or plastic flowers and baskets and containers. Make tissue and paper flowers for the shop.

■ Set up a role-play to reflect a specific experience of a child in the group, such as a wedding, a new baby or a festival such as Hanukkah.

Other curriculum areas

PD Provide opportunities for the children to practise a variety of shoe fastenings, such as buckles, Velcro, laces and slip-ons.

MD Put a variety of shoes and socks in a large pile and invite the children to find matching pairs.

Stepping Stone
Engage in imaginative and role-play based on own first-hand experiences.

Early Learning Goal
Use their imagination in art and design, music, dance, imaginative and role-play and stories.

Group size
Four to six children.

What you need
Posters and advertisements about shoes; empty shoeboxes; tape measures and foot-measuring devices; chairs; old clean shoes; clean pairs of socks.

Preparation
Set out the role-play area as a shoe shop equipped with unused shoeboxes, clean pairs of shoes and socks in various sizes and posters and advertisements for shoes.

Home links
Send home copies of the photocopiable sheet 'What shall I wear?' on page 91 and ask parents and carers to help their child to colour and cut out the eight pictures and to match the footwear with the location.

The doctor's surgery

Early Learning Goal
Use their imagination in art and design, music, dance, imaginative and role-play and stories.

Group size
Four to six children.

What you need
A table; chairs; small camp bed or similar; paper; pencils; telephone; magazines; bandages, stethoscope, play doctor's bag and so on; *Going to the Doctor* by Anne Civardi (Usborne Publishing).

Preparation
Try to organise a visit to your local doctor's surgery. If possible, let the children speak to the receptionist, look at the waiting area and talk to the doctor in their room. Set up a role-play surgery with a waiting area and reception desk in your group.

What to do
■ Read *Going to the Doctor* to the children.
■ Discuss the children's experiences of going to the doctor's. Talk with them about how we make an appointment, what we do while we wait and what is in the doctor's room.
■ Talk about why you might visit the doctor (for a sore throat, upset tummy, bumped heads, bad cuts and so on) and what the doctor does (use a stethoscope to hear breathing, look into your eyes and ears, ask you to stick your tongue out and say 'ah' and so on).
■ Direct the children to the role-play area and encourage them to take on the roles of receptionist, doctor and patients.
■ Take an active role with younger children, participating as a patient or the doctor.
■ Encourage older children to report back after their play, explaining what problem they had and what the doctor's advice or actions were.

More ideas
■ Create an optician's role-play area with spectacle frames (without lenses), mirrors, spectacle cases, an optician's chart and so on.
■ Ask the children to watch cats to see how they move. If possible, video a cat stretching, licking its paws and so on and let the children watch it. Make cat masks and allow them to imitate the movements of a cat. Play music from *Cats* by Andrew Lloyd-Webber (Polydor) as a soundtrack.

Home links
Take photographs of the children involved in the role-play to display or give to carers.

Other curriculum areas
CLL — Provide paper and pens so the children can write prescriptions and let them fill in an 'appointments book'.
PD — Talk about staying healthy by keeping clean, getting enough sleep, having plenty of exercise and healthy food.

Creative development

What a noise!

What to do

- Familiarise yourself with the story.
- Allow the children to have a 'free-play' session with the percussion instruments, investigating their different sounds. Encourage them to play all together to generate a loud noise.
- At this point, put on the crown and assume the role of the music-loving, din-hating queen (or king) from the photocopiable story.
- Call for quiet and ask the children to play individually so that you can decide if you like the sound of their instruments or not. (Of course, you will like them all!)
- Explain how much you love the instruments, but hate the noise that was being made, and ask the children how to make a better noise.
- Help younger children to play their instruments two at a time or to a common beat.
- Encourage older children to think of solutions to the problem by playing their instruments co-operatively.

More ideas

- Place a suitcase and summer clothing in the role-play area, providing the opportunity to plan for a holiday. Encourage the children to discuss where they are going, what they will need and how they are travelling.
- Turn the role-play area into a scene from a nursery rhyme, such as 'Humpty Dumpty' or 'Little Bo Peep' (Traditional).

Stepping Stone
Introduce a story line or narrative into their play.

Early Learning Goal
Use their imagination in art and design, music, dance, imaginative and role-play and stories.

Group size
Up to six children.

What you need
The photocopiable sheet 'The music-loving queen' on page 92; range of percussion instruments; cardboard crown.

Home links
Invite parents and carers to return to the session 15 minutes early to watch the children act out the story while a practitioner reads the narrative aloud.

Other curriculum areas

PSED Read the story 'The music-loving queen' on the photocopiable sheet and discuss how the musicians were making the queen and each other sad. Discuss how agreeing to take turns and to co-operate made everyone happy in the end.

CLL Use a rug as a flying carpet. Provide costumes or props to represent different countries and encourage the children to describe where they have flown too.

Playmats

Play alongside other children who are engaged in the same theme.

Early Learning Goal
Use their imagination in art and design, music, dance, imaginative and role-play and stories.

Group size
Up to four children.

What you need
Large sheet of stiff card; sticky-backed plastic; paint; pens; crayons; tissue paper; glue; modelling materials.

Preparation
Let the children choose a theme, such as 'Pirates', 'The farm' or 'Dinosaurs'.

Home links
Note the children's comments while they are making and using their playmats. Make a display for parents and carers to see, with photographs of the board being made and the final product alongside the children's comments.

What to do
■ Give the children a large sheet of card to make a playmat on their chosen theme.

■ Agree together what features the playmat should have, for example, for a 'Dinosaurs' theme they could include a large lake, a volcano or mountain made from clay or papier mâché, and trees made from stiff paper or play dough.

■ Let the children colour the base using paint, crayons, pencils or by sticking down tissue paper. Once this is dry, cover the flat base by painting on PVA glue.

■ Add any 3-D features using modelling materials.

■ Encourage the children to use the playmat with the appropriate small-world toys.

■ Play alongside younger children, modelling good use of the playmat.

■ Extend the ideas of older children through questioning. For example, 'Where can the small dinosaurs hide from the big one?'.

More ideas
■ Place frieze paper on the floor, prepare brightly coloured paint in trays and make an indoor flower frieze using only handprints and footprints for the leaves and petals. Add stems in black pen when the paint is dry.

■ Invite the children to bring in their teddy bears for a teddy bears' picnic. Lay out picnic rugs and provide snacks.

Other curriculum areas
MD Place toy hard hats beside large wooden blocks and encourage the children to be builders. Count how many blocks each child has used.

KUW Organise a bubble-blowing day outside. Watch bubbles float in the air and get caught on the wind. Talk about their appearance and what happens if you touch them or blow them.

Puppet play

What to do

■ Choose a nursery rhyme or story that the children know well. This could be one that is popular within your group, such as *The Gruffalo*.

■ Support the children in making the different puppets of the characters in the chosen story or rhyme – for example, the mouse, fox, snake, owl and the gruffalo itself for *The Gruffalo*.

■ Show the children how to draw faces for the puppets on card, cut them out and attach them to the back of a wooden spoon. They can add fabric, wool and tissue paper to the 'neck' to represent a body.

■ Once all the puppets are complete gather the children together and seat them in front of the puppet theatre.

■ Perform your chosen story or rhyme using the puppets. If necessary, ask for adult helpers to take part (depending on the complexity of the story and the number of puppets required).

■ Encourage the children to use different voices for the different characters, and model moving the puppets across the 'stage'.

■ Discuss with younger children what a puppet show is all about before they make their characters.

■ Encourage older children to produce their own performance and to show it to an audience of other children.

More ideas

■ Provide simple costumes to help the children act out well-known stories, such as 'Little Red Riding Hood' (Traditional).

■ Sing 'There Were Ten in the Bed' (Traditional) and ask the children to act out the lyrics.

Stepping Stone
Play co-operatively as part of a group to act out a narrative.

Early Learning Goal
Use their imagination in art and design, music, dance, imaginative and role-play and stories.

■

Group size
Up to four children.

■

What you need
Large sheets of cardboard; fabric; wool; tissue paper; wooden spoons; card; paper; pens; crayons; glue; *The Gruffalo* by Julia Donaldson (Macmillan).

■

Preparation
Make a card puppet-theatre frame that could sit on a table draped with fabric, so that the children cannot be seen behind. If appropriate, invest in a commercial theatre or ask parents and carers to help construct a wooden one.

Other curriculum areas

KUW — Tell the story of the Chinese New Year. Make simple masks and let the children act out the animal race.

CLL — Having read and acted out a story, encourage the children to discuss their individual role in the group.

Home links
Inform parents and carers of your intention to make a puppet theatre and ask for volunteers with time or expertise to spare.

All pull together!

What to do

■ Read through the story-book and show the children the illustrations.

■ Discuss how heavy the turnip would have been to pull up. Ask questions to extend the children's understanding, such as, 'Why did the old man ask the old woman to help?' or 'Would any of them have been able to pull up the turnip on their own?'.

■ Ask the children to try to pull something from your grip, such as a beanbag. Keep a firm hold as a child tries to pull it away and point out to the children the way that the child is standing and his or her facial expressions as they exert effort.

■ In a space ask the children to mime pulling a very heavy object. Stress that they should not really pull to avoid falling backwards.

■ Assign roles for the story. If you have more children than characters, create some extra roles.

■ Use very simple props, such as a large beanbag chair to represent the turnip, to help the children get into character.

■ Invite the children to re-enact the whole story.

■ Read the story again for younger children to act alongside, participating in their plan as necessary.

■ Encourage older children to act out the story with perhaps one or two of the more confident children taking the role of narrator.

More ideas

■ Read *The Snowman* by Raymond Briggs (Penguin Books) or show children the video and talk about a snowman coming to life. Pair the children, play the music and let them act out the role of the child and the magical snowman.

Other curriculum areas

KUW During festivals, such as Hanukkah, discuss the traditions and encourage the children to play together as a family celebrating in the role-play area.

PSED Talk about the story of 'The Enormous Turnip' and how it was the smallest of the creatures who made all the difference.

In this chapter, the activities help the children to respond to comments and express themselves in a variety of ways, exploring different types of music, art and drama as well as sharing their ideas and feelings through different forms of communication.

Sensory walk

What to do

▇ Choose an area from your local environment that is easily accessible from your setting, such as a garden, wooded area, street, park, market, beach or a country park.

▇ Prepare the children for taking a walk and organise them into small groups, each with an adult helper and a copy of the worksheet secured to a clipboard.

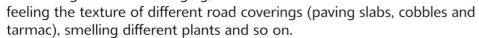

▇ Draw the children's attention to different sensory experiences, such as listening to the birds singing, feeling the texture of different road coverings (paving slabs, cobbles and tarmac), smelling different plants and so on.

▇ Encourage the children to use all of their senses, but remind them not to taste anything!

▇ Provide opportunities for the children to talk about their preferences as they continue on the walk, as well as using facial expressions to show their likes and dislikes.

▇ Use copies of the worksheet and the camera to record the range of stimuli on your walk in your small groups.

▇ Support younger children by drawing their attention to particular stimuli during the walk.

▇ Ask older children to find items that stimulate more than one sense.

More ideas

▇ Create a sensory box containing objects that the children can explore using all of their senses, such as a kaleidoscope, different smelling soaps and so on.

▇ Place a piece of masking tape around the children's wrists, with the sticky side out. Take them on a sensory walk, in the park or wooded area, and encourage them to gather natural objects to attach to their wristbands (without damaging wildlife).

Other curriculum areas

KUW Repeat the sensory walk during different seasons and observe the changes.

CLL Place items that have different textures, shapes or smells in the bottom of old socks and tie them up. Ask the children to work in pairs to match up pictures of the items with the appropriate sock.

Creative development

Senses picture

Early Learning Goal
Respond in a variety of ways to what they see, hear, smell, touch and feel.

■

Group size
Up to ten children.

■

What you need
Lucy's Picture by Nicola Moon (Orchard Books); coloured Cellophane; card; scissors; glue; paints; collage materials; sequins; glitter; sticky stars; feathers; blindfold.

■

Preparation
Make pairs of glasses using cardboard frames and inserting coloured Cellophane for the lenses.

Home links
Ask parents and carers to take their children to visit an optician's and to talk about the different styles of glasses available.

What to do

■ Gather the children in a group and read *Lucy's Picture* to them.

■ Draw the children's attention to the illustrations in the book and discuss how Lucy explains that her grandpa's dog is called Honey because of her colour.

■ Talk with the children about other pets that are given a name because of their colour – for example, Snowball, Patch, Goldie, Ginger, Spot or Snowy.

■ Discuss why Lucy's picture was different from the other children's in the group, and talk about the things that Lucy collected for her picture.

■ Allow the children to gather their own materials like Lucy did in the book and encourage them to make a painting and then a collage.

■ Blindfold the children and allow them to feel the difference between the flat painting and the textured collage.

■ Allow the children to decorate the frames of the cardboard and Cellophane glasses using sequins, stars, glitter and feathers.

■ Encourage the children to try on the different glasses and to talk about the changes in what they can see.

■ Let younger children make one simple collage to feel and compare with their pictures.

■ Invite older children to make a range of different collages and, blindfolded, to feel and identify the different textures.

More ideas

■ Let the children feel an example of Braille. Allow them to make their own Braille messages by placing a sheet of paper on top of a tray of sand and carefully piercing small holes in it with a sharp pencil.

■ Blindfold the children and allow them to explore the room; ensure that the children are carefully supervised by an adult.

Other curriculum areas

PSED Invite someone with a visual impairment in to talk to the group, bringing some examples of Braille and their guide dog.

CLL Set up an optician's shop in the role-play area, placing the pairs of glasses the children have made in the shop.

Creative development

How are you feeling?

What to do

■ Gather the children together in a circle and give each child a copy of the photocopiable sheet.

■ Draw the children's attention to the different expressions on the children's faces.

■ Ask the children which facial expression we would make if someone broke our favourite toy, if someone had said something really nice about us, and so on.

■ Talk about the range of emotions that we can feel at different times.

■ Ask each child in turn which person in the picture they are feeling most like at the moment and why they feel that way.

■ Allow each child to find a space in a large open area.

■ Read out the scenarios from your cards one at a time and allow the children to suggest how someone may feel and respond in that situation.

■ Encourage the children to demonstrate their responses through movement, role-play or mime.

■ Younger children may require some encouragement to mimic facial gestures and body language at first.

■ Invite older children to use body language, gestures and facial expressions to give a personal response to particular scenarios.

More ideas

■ Cut a selection of faces from magazines and glue them on to pieces of card. Talk about the expressions shown and ask the children to imitate some of them.

Other curriculum areas

CLL Use well-known stories, such as 'The Three Billy Goats Gruff' (Traditional), to encourage the children to think about different emotions.

PSED Invite the children to discuss how they thought a certain activity or part of the day went and how they felt at that time.

Stepping Stone
Use body language, gestures, facial expression or words to indicate personal satisfaction or frustration.

Early Learning Goal
Respond in a variety of ways to what they see, hear, smell, touch and feel.

■

Group size
Up to ten children.

■

What you need
The photocopiable sheet 'How do you feel?' on page 94; card; pens.

■

Preparation
Make a copy of the photocopiable sheet for each child.
On pieces of card, make up scenarios that the children can relate to, to allow them to pretend that they are happy, angry and so on – for example, 'What would your mum look like if you gave her a nice present?'.

Home links
Ask parents and carers to play a simple miming game at home to encourage their children to guess from their body language, gestures and facial expressions how they might be feeling.

Happy or sad?

Stepping Stone
Use body language, gestures, facial expression or words to indicate personal satisfaction or frustration.

Early Learning Goal
Respond in a variety of ways to what they see, hear, smell, touch and feel.

Group size
Up to 20 children.

What you need
Just the children.

What to do

■ Gather the children in a circle. Explain to them that they can 'speak' without talking. Invite them to think of ways of saying 'yes' and 'no' with their bodies (they can use their heads or thumbs).

■ Ask questions such as, 'Do you like ice-cream?' and tell the children to respond without speaking.

■ Teach the children the well-known song 'If You're Happy and You Know It' (Traditional) and let them add the actions to the song to show that they are happy.

■ Extend the song to include other emotions and related movements, for example, 'If you're sad and you know it, cry a tear'. Continue with 'tired'/'yawn, yawn'; 'scared'/'cover your eyes'; 'angry'/'stomp your feet'; 'embarrassed'/'hide your face'; 'happy'/'smile and clap'; 'excited'/'jump up and down', and 'love someone'/'blow a kiss'.

■ Give younger children prompts for the movements.

■ Invite the older children to make up their own alternative verses.

More ideas

■ Show the children a picture or photo that reflects an emotion and ask them, 'How is this person feeling?'. Continue by asking, 'Why do you think they are feeling like that?'.

■ Draw pictures showing each of the emotions in the song and place the pictures in a small bag. Invite each child to select a picture and imitate it to the rest of the group, until someone guesses the emotion correctly. Then that child can have a turn.

Home links
Provide parents and carers with a copy of the additional verses so that the children can sing them at home.

Other curriculum areas

MD   Use portraits showing emotions to play a game of 'Snap!'.

CLL   Make a book about body language. Take photos or draw pictures to show how our bodies can talk. Include the following: shoulders shrugging – 'I don't know!'; holding one's nose – 'What a smell!'; holding one's hand up – 'Stop!', and so on.

A windy day

What to do

▓ Read *Windy Day* to the children and talk about the movement caused by the wind in the story. Discuss the sounds, sights and feelings evoked by the windy day.

▓ Help the children to make their own kites following the instructions on the photocopiable sheet and to use pens and crayons to each make patterns on their kites.

▓ Take the children outdoors on a windy day to fly their kites and play in the fallen leaves.

▓ Encourage the children to listen to the sounds they can hear, such as the noise of the kite's tail in the wind and the scrunching and crackling noise as they kick the leaves.

▓ Talk about the movements the kites make and watch what happens when a bundle of dry leaves is thrown up into the air.

▓ Allow the children to explore the texture of different leaves, conkers, cones and seed-heads in the wind.

▓ Support younger children by cutting out and making the kites for them, inviting them to add individual decorations only.

▓ Encourage older children to experiment with different materials to make different kites.

More ideas

▓ Provide pens and pencils for the children to make observational drawings of leaves, cones, conkers or seed-heads.

▓ Let the children experiment with a range of percussion instruments to make sounds that correspond to their experiences of flying kites.

Other curriculum areas

PD Cut pieces of ribbon and tie them to hair 'scrunchies'. Let the children wear these around their wrists and encourage them to carry out a range of movements, waving the ribbons through the air.

KUW Take photographs of the weather each day for a week. Display the photographs and talk about the children's observations.

Stepping Stone
Further explore an experience using a range of senses.

Early Learning Goal
Respond in a variety of ways to what they see, hear, smell, touch and feel.

Group size
Up to ten children.

What you need
The photocopiable sheet 'Make a kite' on page 95; drinking straws; sticky tape; hole-punch; pieces of good quality plastic carrier bags cut into strips (approximately 3cm x 30cm); outdoor clothing; *Windy Day* by Mick Manning and Brita Granström (Franklin Watts); art materials.

Preparation
Make a copy of the photocopiable sheet for each child.

Home links
Ask parents and carers to gather pictures of things that move in the wind, such as hot-air balloons, gliders, kites, windmills, dandelion seeds, sailing boats, wind turbines and so on, to make a display.

Musical moves

Stepping Stone
Begin to use representation as a means of communication.

Early Learning Goal
Express and communicate their ideas, thoughts and feelings by using a widening range of materials, suitable tools, imaginative and role-play, movement, designing and making, and a variety of songs and musical instruments.

Group size
Up to ten children.

What you need
Tape recorder or CD player; tapes or CDs of various types of music; coloured feathers; plastic carrier bags or fabric; margarine-tub lids; sharp scissors (adult use).

Preparation
Make streamers by bending the tub lids in half and cutting out a centre with sharp scissors. Cut pieces of fabric or plastic carrier bags into narrow strips 40cm long. Feed these through the plastic rings that you have created with the lids, and tie the strips in a knot through the ring.

What to do
■ Explain to the children that you are going to play different types of music to them.
■ Allow each child to choose a feather and ask them to find a space on their own.
■ Play your chosen music and encourage the children to keep their feathers in the air by blowing them upwards.
■ Explain that when the music stops the children can stop blowing the feathers.
■ At the end of the session, throw the whole bag of feathers in the air and allow the children to gather up their own collection of feathers as the music plays.
■ To make sure all the feathers are gathered, put the children in groups and ask each group to gather one of the colours of feathers.
■ Next, give the children one of the prepared streamers to move in time with the music, marching and dancing around the room waving their streamers up and down.
■ Let younger children enjoy a period of free play with the feathers and the streamers.
■ Encourage older children to put their movements together in a short sequence, following the rhythm of the music.

More ideas
■ Make a collection of silk and chiffon scarves for the children to twirl and wave as they move around the room to the music.
■ Use craft materials to make different kinds of streamers to move to different types of music.

Home links
Encourage parents and carers to share their music collections with their children at home and to dance and move together.

Other curriculum areas
PSED Invite the children to talk about how music makes them feel (happy, sad, scared, lively and so on).
MD Place several large hoops (three of each colour) around the area. Explain to the children that they should walk around the hoops and that each time the music stops you will call out a colour and they must stand inside a hoop of that colour.

Puppet theatre

What to do

▤ Gather the children around a small table and talk about a recent event that all the children have experienced. Topics may include a recent outing the group went on; what each child's family did at the weekend; coming to the setting this morning; playing with friends; birthdays; seeing a rainbow and so on. Encourage the whole group to share some of their experience of the event.

▤ Focus the discussion on the people or animals that were part of this experience and explain to the children that they are going to make puppets of these people and animals.

▤ Establish whom or what each child has chosen for their story, and provide them with enough envelopes to make their puppets (each envelope can produce two puppets).

▤ Allow the children to cut along the lines of the envelopes, then to draw a character on the front of each triangle that they have cut out. Help each child to fold the corners around and glue or tape them to a size that will fit on their finger (see illustration).

▤ Encourage the children to describe their chosen event with the help of the finger puppets they have produced.

▤ Provide younger children with assistance to make the puppets.

▤ Older children can make more elaborate puppets by adding craft materials, such as wool for hair, felt for eyes and so on.

More ideas

▤ Provide the children with a range of mark-makers and paper so that they can create their own pictures to describe experiences or past actions.

▤ Supply a range of dressing-up clothes and encourage the children to describe experiences or past actions while wearing the clothes.

Other curriculum areas

PSED Provide opportunities for the children to talk about what they have been doing since their last visit to the group. Encourage them to talk about the different things that have happened in their home and their community.

KUW Make picture clue cards, such as a picture of a baby, a picture of someone in an early years setting and so on, for the children to sequence and talk about events in their own lives.

Stepping Stone
Describe experiences and past actions, using a widening range of materials.

Early Learning Goal
Express and communicate their ideas, thoughts and feelings by using a widening range of materials, suitable tools, imaginative and role-play, movement, designing and making, and a variety of songs and musical instruments.
▤
Group size
Up to six children.
▤
What you need
Standard-sized envelopes; felt-tipped pens; glue or sticky tape; scissors.
▤
Preparation
Draw lines on two of the corners of a set of envelopes.

Home links
Let the children take home copies of the photocopiable sheet 'Finger puppets' on page 96 to make simple finger puppets to act out some well-known stories.

Bonfire night

What to do

▪ Gather the children together to look at information books showing pictures of bonfires and fireworks. Talk about why we have fireworks.

▪ Read the poem 'Bonfire Night', then discuss the colours, shapes and sounds that can usually be seen and heard on bonfire nights.

▪ Show the children a video recording of a firework display or listen to sound-effect tapes of fireworks and bonfires and discuss the colours, shapes, smells, movements and noises made.

▪ Divide the children into small groups and invite them to move around the following activities about fireworks.

Song

▪ Use percussion instruments to accompany this song:

Fireworks go snap, snap, snap!
Crack, crack, crack!
Zap, zap, zap!
Fireworks make me clap, clap, clap
On Bonfire Night!

Craft

▪ Make safe sparklers using plastic straws, silver and gold curling ribbon or tinsel. Tape the curled ribbon or tinsel to the ends of the straws and allow the children to move to music with their sparklers.

Art

▪ Make firework pictures by pouring watered-down poster paint on to a paper plate or shallow container. Show the children how to dip toothbrushes into the paint and to bend the bristles back with their fingers on to black construction paper. Sprinkle lightly with glitter for an even more sparkly effect.

More ideas

▪ Provide the children with percussion instruments and encourage them to make firework sound effects.

▪ Use different colours of play dough to make rockets, Catherine wheels, bangers and so on.

Home links
Ask carers to share their experiences of Bonfire nights with their children.

Other curriculum areas

PSED ▪ Use the children's responses as an opportunity to teach them about firework safety.

MD ▪ Adapt the words of the rhyme 'Ten Fat Sausages' (Traditional) to 'Ten loud fireworks glowing in the sky...'.

Creative development

Our art gallery

What to do

■ Gather the children around the display and draw their attention to the beautiful work on show in 'Our art gallery' this week.

■ Invite one of the children to choose a piece of work in the gallery that they think is interesting and to stand up and point to the artwork using a metre stick.

■ Encourage them to ask the child who created the picture questions, such as, 'What did you use to make this piece?', 'What do you like about it now that it is finished?', 'What colours did you use?', 'Did you enjoy making it?', 'What are you going to do with it after it comes down from the gallery?' and so on.

■ Ensure that each child gets the opportunity to have their work displayed in the gallery regularly.

■ Younger children may require an adult to model suitable questions and answers on their behalf.

■ Involve older children in making their own picture frames to display their work.

More ideas

■ Make personal portfolios for the children by hole-punching all their work and placing treasury tags through them to keep them together. The children can then use these as a basis for discussion.

■ At the end of any creative activity, gather the children together in a small group and ask them to reflect on the experience, considering how well they worked as a group, what they enjoyed doing, what they would change next time and so on.

Home links

Invite parents and carers to visit the art gallery and ask questions of the 'artists'.

Other curriculum areas

CLL — Have an 'artist's hot seat' asking a child to sit with one of their pieces of work and to answer questions about it.

MD — Use some of the feedback to make a graph of their favourite colour or medium for working with.

Stepping Stone
Respond to comments and questions, entering into dialogue about their creations.

Early Learning Goal
Express and communicate their ideas, thoughts and feelings by using a widening range of materials, suitable tools, imaginative and role-play, movement, designing and making, and a variety of songs and musical instruments.

Group size
Up to ten children.

What you need
Range of dry pasta shapes; gold powder paint; PVA glue; clip frames; old picture frames; metre stick.

Preparation
Clear an area of wall space and label it 'Our art gallery'. Place the children's creative work in clip frames, old frames or frames made from cardboard with pasta stuck on to it, painted with a mixture of gold powder paint and PVA glue. Display any 3-D creative work, labelled clearly, on a table-top at the children's height.

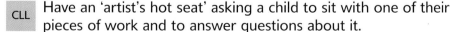

Budding artists

Stepping Stone
Make comparisons.

Early Learning Goal
Express and communicate their ideas, thoughts and feelings by using a widening range of materials, suitable tools, imaginative and role-play, movement, designing and making, and a variety of songs and musical instruments.

Group size
Up to six children.

What you need
Copy of the print *Broadway Boogie-Woogie* by Piet Mondrian (postcards available from art galleries and shops, or visit the website www.art.com); aerial photographs cut from magazines and newspapers; different-sized toy cars; wooden blocks; red, blue and yellow paint in shallow trays; construction paper; sticky paper shapes; boxes.

What to do
■ Show the children some aerial-view photographs cut from magazines and newspapers and ask them if they can recognise anything in the pictures (cars, buildings, gardens, roads, rivers and so on).

■ Show and talk about the print by Mondrian. Explain to the children that this shows what it may be like looking down on streets and buildings from the sky.

■ Talk about the straight lines that the artist uses and the names of the colours in his print. Ask the children to point to the roads and the buildings shown.

■ Invite the children to compare the print to the aerial photographs. Can they see the differences and the similarities?

■ Encourage the children to each make a print in the style of Mondrian by dipping the wheels of the cars into the paint and pushing the car to make tracks on the paper.

■ Show them how to dip the wooden blocks into the shallow trays of paint and to use them to print the buildings.

■ When the prints are dry, encourage the children, once again, to make comparisons. This time ask them to comment on the similarities and differences between their print and that of Mondrian's.

■ Younger children could make a picture in the style of Mondrian by sticking sticky shapes on to a sheet of paper.

■ Older children could make a 3-D Mondrian-style sculpture by painting boxes red, blue and yellow and setting them out like a city scene.

More ideas
■ Share the book *Katie Meets the Impressionists* by James Mayhew (Orchard Books) with the children. Talk about the Impressionists' style of painting and what Katie saw in the book. Create your own Impressionist-style pictures and compare them to those in the book.

Home links
Ask parents and carers to take their children on a visit to an art gallery or museum. Many have children's trails that are suitable for young children.

Other curriculum areas
KUW Use drawing programs on the computer to make pictures in the style of Mondrian.

MD Look at different examples of Mondrian's prints and name the different shapes.

Creative development

These final activities relate to specific Stepping Stones, but can be adapted to any area of Creative development. They help the children to provide open-ended responses, the focus being on the processes that they are going through, rather than the response that they produce.

Pick and mix

Stepping Stone
Develop preferences for forms of expression.

What to do

■ Organise all the areas in your setting so that the children can access them freely, ensuring that all the equipment and resources are accessible to the children.

■ Set up a trolley or tray with musical instruments that the children can choose from.

■ Clear an area that the children can use for creative movement or dancing.

■ Clearly label all the art and craft materials and make sure that they are at the children's height. Label storage boxes with appropriate pictures and words.

■ Set up a clothes rail with different outfits in the role-play area. Provide a box or suitcase of props that the children can use and adapt for their play experiences.

■ An environment such as this one, where the children can respond spontaneously, will enable them to develop preferences for forms of expression rather than stifled adult-led responses.

■ Children need to be actively encouraged to represent their ideas in different ways and, therefore, should be given stretches of uninterrupted time to explore and express their own ideas.

■ Children's responses should be spontaneous. For example, after listening to a story or singing a song about 'spring', some children may want to make flowers from straws and tissue paper. Another group of children may choose to dig and plants bulbs in the sand tray, while another child may wish to use wooden blocks to make flowers.

More ideas

■ Celebrate the diversity of the children's creative responses by drawing them together at the end of the session to talk about what they did. This may help other children with ideas for future activities.

■ Encourage the children to help you tidy materials away to encourage a sense of ownership in the room.

Early Learning Goal
Express and communicate their ideas, thoughts and feelings by using a widening range of materials, suitable tools, imaginative and role-play, movement, designing and making, and a variety of songs and musical instruments.

■

Group size
Whole group.

■

What you need
Activity areas throughout your setting organised so that the children can access them freely.

Other curriculum areas

CLL Let the children help make the labels for the different resources throughout the setting.

PSED Make badges for each area so that the children know the maximum number of children allowed to play in each area at a time.

Home links
Work with parents and carers to value the creative processes that their children go through, as well as the results that they achieve.

Bags of ideas

Stepping Stone
Talk about personal intentions, describing what they were trying to do.

Early Learning Goal
Express and communicate their ideas, thoughts and feelings by using a widening range of materials, suitable tools, imaginative and role-play, movement, designing and making, and a variety of songs and musical instruments.

Group size
Whole group.

What you need
An attractive bag or box and a wide selection of resources and materials from around the setting, for example: a pair of scissors, ingredients for making play dough, marker pens, a tambourine, a cassette of African music, a pot from the role-play corner and so on.

Preparation
Gather a range of items from around the room that may be used in creative development activities and place these in an attractive bag or box.

What to do
- Gather the children in a circle and place the bag or box in the centre.
- Select one of the items and ask the children what they could do with it, in which area they would use it and whether or not they would like to use it today.
- Pick another item out and ask for ideas.
- Allow the children to take turns to select something from the box or bag themselves.
- Encourage them to say what the item is called, what it is used for, who may use it and how they would use it.
- By presenting the materials in this way, you will help the children to formulate a plan for the day or part of the day.
- When the children have selected an activity, engage with them to encourage them to talk about what they are doing.
- Vary the items used and change the collection often.

More ideas
- Cover crisp tubes with construction paper and attach a label stating the name of a play area. Add a suitable picture, for example, a paintbrush for the art area, a drum for the music area and so on. Then write the children's names on small cards and add a symbol on each card to help the children recognise their name cards. Encourage the children to post their cards in the appropriate tubes to help them select their activities for the day.

Home links
Let parents and carers know which activity areas their child has been working in so that they can ask their child what they were trying to do there.

Other curriculum areas
CLL Make simple storyboards with the children. Scribe for them so that they can record what they want to do, how they are going to do it and what they will need.

KUW Make a plan of the setting on a large sheet of paper clearly showing the different activity areas. Give each child a car and let them park their car in the area on your plan that they intend playing in next.

News time

What to do

■ After completing any creative activities, such as artwork, movement, craftwork, musical or role-play, gather the children in a circle.

■ Invite the children to bring with them a piece of equipment or piece of work from the area where they have been playing.

■ Ask an adult to pretend to be a news reporter that has come to speak to the children. They should state where they are reporting from (name of your setting), their name and the names of the people that they are going to be interviewing.

■ To fully engage the children, give them titles such as 'Mr Simon Keilty' or 'Miss Susie Ho'.

■ Start the interview by saying, 'Mr Keilty, can you tell us about where you were working today?'.

■ Offer the microphone to the child for their response. Some children will respond freely, others will need a lot of encouragement and questions.

■ When one child has completed the interview, ask them to choose who should be interviewed next.

■ Younger children may require more prompting and encouragement to offer any input.

■ Older children could take on the role of being the reporter.

More ideas

■ Provide other props that will encourage the children to talk, such as a toy phone, walkie-talkie, megaphone or a mobile phone, and let them choose which one to talk through.

■ At the end of a session select pieces of the children's work for the group to look at. Model questions until the children become confident to ask their own questions of one another.

Stepping Stone
Respond to comments and questions, entering into dialogue about their creations.

Early Learning Goal
Express and communicate their ideas, thoughts and feelings by using a widening range of materials, suitable tools, imaginative and role-play, movement, designing and making, and a variety of songs and musical instruments.

■

Group size
Up to six children.

■

What you need
A toy microphone; materials from creative play areas.

Other curriculum areas

KUW Allow the children to use a tape recorder to record their dialogues and discussions about their work.

CLL Decorate a chair and call it the 'Hot seat'. Invite the children to sit on it to show and talk about pieces of work that they have made, responding to questions from their peers and adults in the setting.

Home links
Ask parents and carers to let the children see the news on television in order to watch a news reporter.

Creative development

Musical moments

Stepping Stone
Make comparisons.

Early Learning Goal
Express and communicate their ideas, thoughts and feelings by using a widening range of materials, suitable tools, imaginative and role-play, movement, designing and making, and a variety of songs and musical instruments.

■

Group size
Up to ten children.

■

What you need
Recording of one of the following pieces of music: *The Sorcerer's Apprentice* by Dukas; *The Nutcracker Suite* by Tchaikovsky or *The Rite of Spring* by Stravinsky; video of *Fantasia* (Disney); video recorder; camcorder.

■

Preparation
Listen to the piece of music and find the matching piece in the *Fantasia* video.

Home links
Encourage parents and carers to listen to classical music at home with their children.

What to do
■ Play the selected piece of music and talk about its title. Ask the children to consider why it has been given that name. Ask the children what the music reminds them of.

■ Play the piece of music again and let the children move around the room, creating movements as they go.

■ Gather the children together to discuss the types of movement they made. Ask for volunteers to demonstrate some of their movements to the whole group.

■ In another session, explain to the children that you want them to move to the music again and that you will be recording them as they move. Video-tape their movements and then play the video back to them.

■ Explain to the children that the chosen piece of music is in the video *Fantasia* and show them the excerpt. Discuss the movements that they see in the video.

■ Encourage the children to make comparisons between the movements that they made themselves and those seen in the video of *Fantasia*.

■ Help younger children to describe what the music makes them think of.

■ Older children can work in small groups to make up their own sequences of movements to music.

More ideas
■ Repeat the activity using classical music and the video of *Barbie in the Nutcracker* (Universal Pictures Video) or *Peter and the Wolf* (Sanctuary Digital Entertainment).

■ Invite a local ballet or opera company to work alongside the children.

Other curriculum areas
PSED Play classical music as a signal for the children to tidy up the activities that they have been working on and to come together for circle time. Ask the children which pieces of music they like or dislike and encourage them to make comparisons.

KUW Play pieces of music from a range of cultures to the children and show them pictures of some of the instruments being used in the pieces.

Creative development

Creative development

Name _____

Goals	Assessment	Date
Explore colour, texture, shape, form and space in two or three dimensions.		
Recognise and explore how sounds can be changed, sing simple songs from memory, recognise repeated sounds and sound patterns and match movements to music.		
Use their imagination in art and design, music, dance, imaginative and role-play and stories.		
Respond in a variety of ways to what they see, hear, smell, touch and feel.		
Express and communicate their ideas, thoughts and feelings by using a widening range of materials, suitable tools, imaginative and role-play, movement, designing and making, and a variety of songs and musical instruments.		

Gloop and papier mâché

To make gloop

■ Mix four cups of cornflour with four cups of water. Add food colouring. Pour the mixture into a large tray for the children to explore.

Add more cornflour or water to vary the consistency of the mixture.

■ Mix four cups of flour, one cup of sugar, one cup of salt and two cups of water. Sift the flour and mix it with the salt and sugar. Gradually add the water, stirring it with a whisk or wooden spoon until the mixture is smooth. Add food colouring.

To make papier mâché

■ Combine half a cup of flour with two cups of cold water in a bowl. Add this mixture to a saucepan of two cups of boiling water and bring it to the boil again. Remove from the heat and stir in three tablespoons of sugar. Let it cool; it will thicken as it cools. Once it does, it is ready to use.

■ For a quick and easy papier-mâché paste, simply mix up a box of powdered wallpaper paste (look for the non-toxic label) with water according to the directions on the box. Add some PVA glue to make it more adhesive.

■ Make papier-mâché pulp by placing several sheets of used paper, toilet tissue, paper towel or newspaper (torn into tiny pieces) into a blender or food processor with some water. Strain the pulp using a colander or sieve. Mix the pulp with PVA glue until it has a sticky consistency.

Photocopiable

Creative development

Play-dough recipes

Play dough

Mix two cups of flour, one cup of salt and two tablespoons of cream of tartar together. Add two cups of water and two tablespoons of baby oil and stir well. Place in a microwave on 'high' for four to five minutes. Stir and then microwave for a further minute. Repeat until the mixture has the consistency of mashed potato. When the mixture is cool enough to touch, knead it.

Oatmeal dough

Mix one cup of flour, two cups of oatmeal and one cup of water. Add the water gradually to the flour and oatmeal in a bowl. Knead the mixture together. Add food essences to give an aroma.

Gingerbread dough

Mix two cups of flour, one cup of salt, two teaspoons of ground cinnamon, one teaspoon of ground cloves and one cup of water.

   Use this recipe to make ornaments or decorations. Use the dough to mould in the usual way and open out a paper clip and insert it into the ornament as a hook. Leave to dry.

Coffee dough

Dissolve a quarter cup of instant coffee in one and a half cups of warm water. In another bowl mix four cups of flour and one cup of salt.

   Make a hole in the mixture and add one cupful of the coffee water. Mix with your hands until smooth. Add more of the coffee water until the mixture is smooth and satiny.

Fruit dough

Mix a pack of jelly crystals with two cups of flour, one cup of salt and four tablespoons of cream of tartar in a pan. Add two cups of boiling water and two tablespoons of cooking oil and stir over a medium heat until the mixture forms a ball. Allow to cool.

Paint recipes

Glimmer paint

Mix half a cup of salt, half a cup of flour, half a cup of water and food colouring to create paint that will glimmer when dry.

Glossy paint

Mix four tablespoons of golden syrup with one and a half teaspoons of washing-up liquid to poster paint. This is good for festive themes.

Shiny paint

Mix cornflour with powder paint to make a thick, shiny paint.

Salt paint

Mix table salt with poster paint for a thick, sandy paint, which creates interesting textures as it dries.

Sticky paint

Mix five cups of water, two cups of plain flour, half a cup of sugar and three tablespoons of salt together. Pour the mixture into a saucepan and cook for about seven minutes over a medium heat, until the mixture is thick and bubbling. Allow the mixture to cool.

Add food colouring or poster paint to make different colours. Make the paint more sensory by adding aromas such as strawberry essence, ground cinnamon, lemon essence and so on.

Store this mixture in an airtight container in the fridge for up to two weeks.

Invisible paint

Mix four tablespoons of bicarbonate of soda with four tablespoons of water. Allow the children to paint with this mixture using cotton buds. Leave to dry. Cover with thin watercolours to reveal the 'invisible' picture.

Scented paint

Add jelly crystals to poster paint. Add cherry or strawberry to red paint; lime to green paint; lemon to yellow paint and so on.

Space creatures

Play-dough shapes

Can you make these shapes?

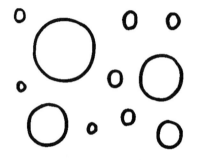

ball shapes　　　　worm shapes　　　　spiral shapes

Can you use some of these to make shapes and marks in your play dough?

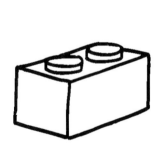

building bricks　　　　keys　　　　nuts and bolts

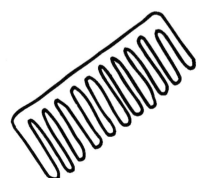

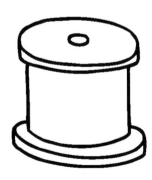

biscuit cutters　　　　combs　　　　cotton reels

Make your mark

Copy these patterns then make up some of your own.

Photocopiable

I like to... to music

Colour the parts of the body that you can move to music. Tell a grown-up how you like to move that part and they will write it down.

hands	knees
shoulders	head	neck
hips	arms	feet

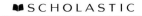

Round the zoo

Round, round, round the zoo   *(Hold hands and dance in a circle.)*
Round and round all day
Until we see a zebra
Who wants to come and play.

Gallop, gallop, gallop   *(Drop hands and gallop round in a circle.)*
The fastest you can do
Just like the zebra
Living at the zoo.

Repeat first verse using 'monkey'.   *(Hold hands and dance in a circle.)*

Scamper, scamper, scamper   *(Scamper on the spot swinging arms.)*
The best that you can do
Just like the monkey
Living at the zoo.

Repeat first verse using 'crocodile'.   *(Hold hands and dance in a circle.)*

Snap, snap, snap your jaws   *(Stand still, snap hands like jaws.)*
The widest you can do
Just like the crocodile
Living at the zoo.

Repeat first verse using 'giraffe'.   *(Hold hands and dance in a circle.)*

Stretch, stretch, stretch your neck   *(Walk on tiptoe, stretching neck.)*
The highest you can do
Just like a tall giraffe
Living at the zoo.

Brenda Williams

Creative development   **Photocopiable**

■ SCHOLASTIC

Make a sound story

Draw a line to link each picture with the instruments that would make the matching sound.

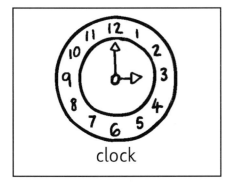

clock

fairy

horse

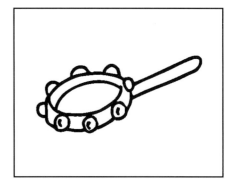

thunderstorm

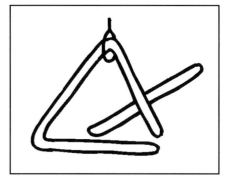

Who will I be?

Put on a crown, who will I be?
A royal king is what you will see

Put on a helmet, who will I be?
A smart policeman is what you will see

Put on a pointy hat, who will I be?
A magical wizard is what you will see

Put on a hard-hat, who will I be?
A hard-working builder is what you will see

Put on a head-dress, who will I be?
An Indian chief is what you will see

Put on a cowboy hat, who will I be?
A sheriff brave is what you will see

I put on a hat and can change who I'll be
But under the hat, of course, I'm still me.

Susan Smith

Goldilocks

Goldilocks walked through the forest,	(Children walk around in circle.)
And found the house of the bears,	
She knocked on the door and went inside,	(Knocking motion.)
But nobody was there,	
In the kitchen were three bowls of porridge,	(Hold up three fingers.)
But the big one was really too hot,	(Pretend to blow.)
One was too cold but the small one was fine,	
And so she ate up the lot.	(Mime eating with spoon.)
She then spotted three chairs to sit on,	
And so upon each one she sat,	(Make as if to sit.)
But the big one was hard, the middle one soft,	
And the small one, well it just fell flat,	(Loud clap on 'flat'.)
Goldilocks felt very tired now,	(Yawn and stretch.)
And decided to climb up the stairs,	(Mime climbing stairs.)
And that's where she found the bedroom,	
Of the family of the Three Bears,	(Hold up three fingers.)
The first bed was hard, the second one soft,	
So into the third one she crept,	(Mime creeping motion.)
It was so lovely and warm there,	
That she closed her eyes and she slept,	(Close eyes, rest head on hands.)
The Three Bears were cross when they got home,	(Hands on hips, angry faces.)
Because of the mess that they found,	
Then upstairs they ran waking Goldilocks up,	(Mime running.)
With a terrible growling sound,	(Make growling noises.)
Goldilocks jumped off the bed then,	
She'd been given a terrible fright,	
She ran down the stairs as fast as she could,	(Mime running.)
And disappeared right out of sight,	
Mummy and Daddy Bear smiled,	(Smile.)
They gave a big sigh and a shrug,	(Sigh and shrug shoulders.)
Then Baby Bear came up beside them,	
And gave them a lovely big hug.	(Hug person next to you.)

Susan Smith

What shall I wear?

Colour and cut out the pictures. Match them together.
When would you wear your wellington boots?

Photocopiable

The music-loving queen

Once there was a queen who loved music. She lived in a huge palace, but as she had no family, it seemed a very empty and lonely place. During the day the queen's servants were around, but in the evenings the palace was very quiet indeed. The queen did not like it.

One day she told her royal advisor how unhappy she was.

'Ah, Your Majesty', said her advisor, 'you love music, so perhaps you should organise to have musicians come here in the evenings to play for you. That way it wouldn't be so quiet and you wouldn't be on your own.'

The queen thought this was a brilliant idea. A royal messenger was sent out to the nearby towns and villages, asking musicians to go to the palace and play for the queen. Many people turned up at the palace the very next day, all wanting to play for the queen.

The queen was very excited. 'I do love music,' she said. 'Ask them to gather in the great hall so I can listen to them play.' All the musicians went to the great hall. There were people with horns, people with shakers, people with drums, people with flutes and people with tambourines. In fact, almost any instrument you can think of was there in the great hall.

'Right,' said the queen. 'Play for me, please.'

All at once there was a thunderous din. The queen covered her ears and shouted, 'STOP!!'

She couldn't understand where the terrible noise was coming from, but this was not music and she did not like it at all. She decided that someone must have brought a dreadful instrument that she had never seen or heard before, so she asked them to play one by one until this awful instrument could be found.

Each of the musicians played. By the time she'd heard the last instrument she was very puzzled indeed. 'You all sound wonderful, yet when you play together, there is a terrible noise that hurts my ears. How can this be?'

She called for the royal advisor and asked what could be done.

'Your Majesty,' the advisor said, 'they must have a plan to follow to make music. Perhaps they could each play at different times, or some of them play together to a set beat.'

On hearing this, the musicians began to work together, taking turns and not all trying to be the loudest. The sound was wonderful. The queen was very happy indeed and her evenings were never quiet or lonely again.

Susan Smith

Photocopiable

Creative development

The enormous turnip

Cut out these pictures and put them in the correct order.

■SCHOLASTIC

How do you feel?

Photocopiable

Creative development

Make a kite

1. Cut out along the thick line and fold along the dotted lines.
2. Use a hole-punch to punch the ○ when folded together.
3. Staple the **X**s together, ensuring that the middle fold comes towards you.
4. Attach 1m of string through the punched holes.
5. Attach a strip of plastic-bag material between the **Y**s and staple together.

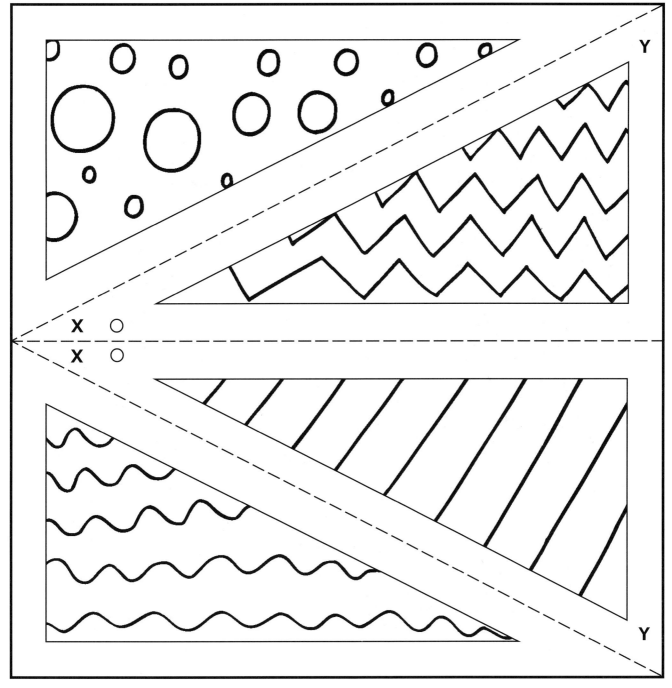

Finger puppets

fold and glue 	fold and glue 
fold and glue 	fold and glue 
fold and glue 	fold and glue 
fold and glue 	fold and glue 

Photocopiable

Creative development